How

Your Home a

Smart Home

Smart Home

Professor

Stuart Hamilton

This book is dedicated to all those people who wander into stores or browse online and see all kinds of cool electronics and think that it's too complicated for them to learn how to use or install themselves. I empathize with you one hundred per cent because I am married to a wonderful person who might be just like you. Having spent a twenty plus years in the complex and ever-changing world of computer networking, I made a career out of simplifying complicated matters so anyone could understand them. I did the dry runs and made the mistakes myself so that others would be spared both the time and the expense.

It is my hope that the purchase of this book will save you both time and money as you begin or continue your Smart Home journey. Because many things will change over time, there is a website at www.smarthomeprofessor.com where you can get updates on new developments.

Acknowledgements

Writing a book like this is truly a team effort and I deeply appreciate all the interest and input from a wide variety of people.

The best advice on authoring a book often comes from those who have done it before and have a proven track record. I would like to thank book authors Jim Doherty, Curt Pesmen, and Andrew Friedman for taking the time to talk with me and offer their valuable advice. I also appreciate the time with Mary Beth Ray from Pearson Publishing for her advice on the publishing side.

It's sometimes hard to know where to find people willing to give industry insider advice, and so thanks to the people who helped point me in their direction. Mary Gorges, Jack Neary, Matt Van Tuinen, and Jim Doherty.

A book can't really be reviewed enough and I truly valued the input I got from Gene Arantowicz, Curt Pesmen, Mitchell Allen, Liza Ruff, Steve Haber, and my wife, Joanne Hamilton, who always drives me to keep things simple, puts up with all my technology tinkering, chose the color scheme for the cover, and most importantly provides her ongoing encouragement and moral support. Also special thanks to Maureen Scott for knocking out the last set of typos and grammar issues.

Lastly, and most importantly, a huge debt of gratitude to Michael Redhill, an accomplished author and wonderful editor who took my rather mundane and repetitive prose and made the words dance and sing. I even left in some of your jokes!

Table of Contents

Summary 223

Introduction

Do you have a smartphone? If you do, then you already have the most important component of your Smart Home in your pocket. (If you don't, you should really think of getting one!) This book is for people who are thinking about making their home a Smart Home, might not know exactly what that means, but can use their smartphone as more than a telephone or a paperweight.

I had the inspiration for writing this book about a year ago when I was wandering in a local hardware store. There was a beautiful display of Smart Home products as cool and appealing as anything you'd see in an Apple store. Products for automatic lighting, robot vacuums, video cameras, security systems, and just about everything else you could think of, and they all had one thing in common: you could fully operate all of these home systems through your smartphone. These new gadgets connected to the Internet through your home network and you could operate them from your smartphone whether you were at home or in Timbuktu.

This is an awesome and daunting opportunity for a homeowner. Imagine automating your home! Until now, this was a futuristic sort of fantasy, but as I could see from scanning the shelves, it was finally possible. I wondered, however, how easy it would really be to set up your house out and get it all to work together in a way that you, your spouse and others could use without becoming a tech expert? So, I set out to do what you may not have the time or expertise to do: make it *really easy* to transform your home into the most modern and efficient house on the block. I made some mistakes along the way, but you won't make the same ones. And you don't need a professional installer, either. All that is needed is you, a smartphone, the products you want to install and you will be off to the races.

The other twist is that during the writing of this book we sold our Smart Home and moved into another house that could best be described as a clean slate, technology-wise. In the process of transferring my old Smart Home setup to the buyer of our house, I learned some hard lessons about what not to do and I also made some different decisions in my selections for the new house. You may not be thinking of moving any time soon, but I learned a few tricks to make the transfer of Smart Home control much simpler, and all of these techniques appear as asides throughout the book, and chapter 19 treats the subject fully.

The book is divided into three parts. Part A covers the basics of setting up a home network so that it's ready for Smart Home products.   I explain how to easily test your network for every location you want to put a Smart Home product, and also simple ways to deal with passwords and regular backups.

Part B shows a couple of practical uses of your home network for streaming music and managing your photos. I've had multiple people who visited my Smart Home ask how we're doing that so I included a short section to help you easily enjoy both of those.

Part C covers ten different Smart Home solutions with some strategies for how to make them work together. In this part, I also discuss how to make moving into or out of a Smart Home a smooth experience.

If you want quick answers to any of these Smart Home solutions, you can skip to the end of each chapter to read "The Bottom Line" on each technology area. It tells you what I bought, how much to budget, and the end result.

Because I actually installed and use everything that is described in this book, and I have an iPhone, many of the examples involve the inherent simplicity of using Apple products and Apple HomeKit compatible devices. That said, there is plenty of information in this book about what options an Android user has to achieve similar goals.

How to Use this Book

Most people have home networks and can probably start to put in some of the cool technology solutions described in Part C of the book right away. Please feel free to jump ahead and do this knowing that with a properly built network in place, all of these Smart Home solutions can work along with all the other things you are probably already doing on your home WiFi network.

If you want to get all the basics in place, start at Part A. People who have had poor experiences with Smart Home products are likely to have a poor or inadequate network in place. Setting up your network properly may not be the most exciting part of this book, but it is the foundation of your Smart Home.

All of the products and technology mentioned in this book are subject to a rapidly changing market. I'll keep you up to date on the latest through my website, www.smarthomeprofessor.com.

Although I have chosen specific products to use as examples in this book, I paid for everything myself and did not receive any payment, compensation or input from any of the companies mentioned.

If you decide to copy everything that is covered in this book, it is likely, but not guaranteed, that you will get the same results that I did. I encourage you to use the techniques that you will learn in this book to customize your

Smart Home experience to your specific needs. Whether you decide to tackle it all, add on slowly, or just do the parts that are relevant to you, this book will provide valuable money and time-saving tips. Always remember that products, software, and entire companies change, so always consult the online resources available to make sure you have the latest information.

What a Smart Home Should Do

It should be automatic, at home or away

When you add a Smart Home device, you should be able control it from inside the home when your smartphone is on your home WiFi network, or from anywhere else, as long as you have a cellular signal. Automation is a key component of Smart Home systems, and you should be able to set automatic timers for lighting, heating and cooling, window coverings, or any other Smart Home product.

It works the old way too

Even though you'll want to use your smartphone to make your Smart Home perform, it's always nice to also be able to walk up to a light switch or thermostat and use it the traditional way. When you have guests over, it might not even be apparent to them that you have a Smart Home and that's a good thing because it will save you time explaining how to download an app to go the bathroom.

It should be easy to install

All devices should be simple to install for anybody, even if they have no technical experience.   You may still choose to hire an electrician if you are not comfortable with wiring for example, but all the setup and programming is easily within any smartphone owner's ability.

It should function on a simple network

The first part of this book is dedicated to setting up your home network.   If you follow the steps with the same products that I used or similar ones from other vendors, your network will be ready for the Smart Home products used in this book.   You don't have to know anything about networking to be successful getting your network up and running, and you can do it yourself.

Use a minimum number of smartphone apps

In an ideal world, you'd only have to download one phone app to set up and run all of the Smart Home products that you want to use. But this is not an ideal world, so for now you will need to download and run the app that is appropriate for the installation of each device, but you should be able to *operate* your home system through a much smaller number of apps. The trickiest part of the Smart Home project is that the technology is constantly evolving and a one-app solution, while getting closer, is still in the future. But it will arrive, and when it does, life will only get simpler. For the time being, there exists only a next-to-perfect but highly functional solution for full-home automation.

Your family should love it

A Smart Home should be intuitive and easy to use for your entire family. Remember, they live there, too! Luckily, once you're finished reading this book and installing your devices, the family cat should be able to dim the lights. The goal of this book is to make your Smart Home fun and accessible for *everyone.*

Minimal or no monthly fees

Some vendors want to charge you a monthly fee to operate a device, for instance to retrieve video snippets. With the exception of paying a (low) monthly fee for your security system monitoring, your goal should be to minimize or eliminate any monthly ongoing fees. I offer in this book a good range of products and manufacturers who do not charge ongoing fees. If you want to go beyond what I suggest here, you may encounter fees for use.

It should be reliable

Any time new technology comes out, early adopters run the risk of paying steeply for products that will likely need to be upgraded until it reaches a more stable state. I have aimed to point the reader toward products that will not need to be frequently upgraded and will just work day-to-day.

It should be secure

It is impossible to take every device and every service you buy and evaluate how hackable it is. The only thing you can do is practice good online hygiene by setting up your network in the most secure way possible, choosing difficult passwords and buying from vendors who have a lot to lose if their products are hacked.

As we go through the different sections of the book, you may want to refer back to this set of goals. I will be forthright with you about my assessment of whether these goals are met with the solutions that I chose for my Smart Home. Also, your goals may be different, so take a moment to write them down and it will make it easier to select which products to become the foundation of your Smart Home.

Part A - The Basics

If you have some Smart Home devices working already or just can't wait to try some, it is fine to jump ahead to Part C and add more. If you run into trouble with connectivity or stability, you can come back to this section and make adjustments to your Internet and home network to ensure you have a stable platform for your Smart Home investment.

I know that I have certainly been in this situation before and maybe you have too: I once laid down some interlocking patio stones in the pre You-Tube days and spent quite a bit of time leveling the dirt below before placing the bricks. It looked great for the first month or so, but things like rain, frost, and weeds made me go back, rip it out and start over again, this time doing it the correct way with the proper foundation in place. We don't want to repeat this mistake with your Smart Home Project.

In the Smart Home world, things like video cameras, doorbells, devices tucked away in far corners, and even what your neighbors have set up, can all influence the overall success of your project in ways you may not anticipate. The contents of this section will go through in detail how to set up your underlying network and security environment to ensure that you don't run into any of these road bumps.

Chapter 1 – Internet Access

Without Internet access in your home, you won't have a functioning Smart Home. The type of Internet access we are talking about is the one used in your home, usually provided by either your phone or cable company. (This is different than the data on your smartphone which only serves your smartphone) The home Internet access will be used and shared by all of the Internet-aware devices in your home including your smartphone and Smart Home products, so it's important — although not difficult — to get this set up correctly, securely, and reliably.

There are three distinct segments to your Internet access, two of which you have some control over and one that you don't, but you can measure them together to get a pretty good indication of how well your overall network is working.

To break Internet access into its three segments, imagine you're connecting over your WiFi to smarthomeprofessor.com on your laptop. The first part of that connection is between your laptop and the wireless router in your home. You have a great amount of control over this segment of the connection and the next chapter will

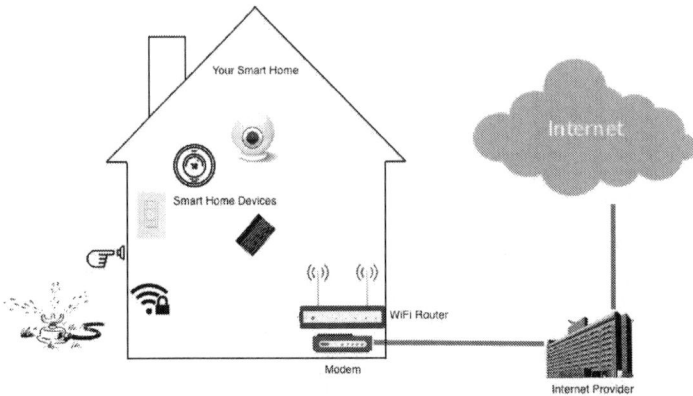

cover this in detail. The second segment is from your router to your Internet Service Provider (ISP). You also have control over this segment, as this represents the service you order from your ISP. That is the subject of this chapter. The third and final segment is from your ISP to smarthomeprofessor.com — or anywhere else on the Internet you might be going. You have no control over this third segment, and unless there is a major Internet malfunction, it will rarely be the source of a bad connection.

> If you remember only one thing from this chapter, remember that your overall performance is determined by the WORST of the three segments.

Each of the three segments can be thought of independently, so if you set things up the best way you can on the segments you control, you'll get the best overall experience and throughput, often referred to as speed or data rate. You can have great Internet service from your home to the ISP and the Internet itself is performing well but if your wireless network is running poorly, your Smart Home will reflect that. By controlling the two segments you *can* control, you will maximize your Smart Home experience. Later I'll explain how to measure performance and how to get the network in your home to possibly outperform your ISP's service.

When shopping for Internet access, the main thing to look at are the possible upload and download speeds available from the provider. Upload speed is the speed at which data from your home leaves your house and goes somewhere on the Internet. Download speed is the opposite; it measures the speed at which data comes from the Internet into your home. Most often people have much higher download speeds than upload and that's because doing things like watching Netflix, checking e-mail, and visiting web sites all bring data into your home

> Mbps means Megabits per second. To put this in perspective, streaming a High Definition Netflix movie to play on your TV would require a download speed of about 5Mbps.

rather than sending it to the Internet, such as when you upload a picture to Instagram.

How much is enough? As an example, I have Comcast Internet service from the cable company and although multiple service offerings were available, ours has a measured download speed of 110Mbps and an upload speed of 6Mbps. It is interesting to note that my service is called "Performance Pro" and is rated for (guaranteed to have) 75Mbps down and 5Mbps up so I am getting better than the stated specifications.

Obviously the higher the download and upload speeds, the better, but it does come at a cost. If you can get it in your area, I would try to keep the download speeds well above 10Mbps (50Mbps or above is ideal) and upload speeds of 2Mbps or greater (5Mbps or more is ideal). If you plan on having Internet cameras in your home, you will want the upload speed to be even higher. Of course, it is always good to know for yourself that you are getting what you're paying for, so I'll show you later how to test this.

There are three kinds of wiring that come into your house that can be used to provide Internet service. The cable company will typically use coaxial cable, which makes very high speeds possible. (Coaxial is the round cable with one wire sticking out of the middle which screws into your TV cable connection.) The phone company can use the same phone wires that your traditional home phone is plugged into (they call these wires "twisted pair"), and the speeds will vary quite a bit depending on how far away your house is from the other end of those wires. Just because someone on your street gets great service, doesn't mean you will, so check and verify with the service provider before signing any kind of contract. This technology is typically called DSL (or Digital Subscriber Line). Often the speed with DSL is lower than with cable but the ISP will tell you that you have a dedicated connection. Cable is a shared connection with your neighbors. Again, I have used cable for many years and DSL before that, so it usually boils down to price and performance. The third option that may be available in your area is fiber and this will almost always offer the highest speeds. If the price is reasonable, you should definitely look at this option but make sure that you have the option to use your own router to set up WiFi.

I am a strong advocate of buying and owning your own router rather than renting one from the service provider. I know this can sound kind of scary if you don't know the first thing about routers and WiFi, but read on and not only will you see why this is a good idea but you will also be able to install it and make it work yourself. Most importantly, it will give you superior stability, a much smaller physical device, the ability to do complete home WiFi coverage, and probably save you on monthly fees.

A newer trend for ISPs is to count the amount of data used by adding both the data coming in and going out over your monthly service period. These so-called data caps usually mean that you have to pay extra if you go over the limit (which can vary depending on the speed of Internet service). Many of the Smart Home devices won't contribute too much towards that data limit with the notable exception of anything to do with video, like cameras and video doorbells. Watching a lot of Netflix or other streaming services can also be a big contributor. It's important to monitor your data use so you can stay within your limits, or to learn that you need to increase them. Later in the security system section, some detail is provided on how much of an impact video cameras can have on your data usage.

All the technical knowledge you need ...

No matter what your level of technical knowledge or ability, by the time you've read this section, you'll have everything you need to know to make all your network equipment work.

WiFi

You have probably heard of this since every computer, smartphone, tablet and many other devices have WiFi. But what is it and what do you need to know about it? Strangely, no one can agree on what "WiFi" stands for. It's generally understood that the "wi" is for wireless, but apparently, the "fi" doesn't stand for anything. Most people think it's just meant to rhyme with "HiFi," in which the "fi" stood for fidelity. But "wireless fidelity" is not a thing. Suffice it to say that WiFi is the standard method of connecting to the Internet at home, at work, and in public. A small WiFi radio in your phone, computer, or other device that uses the internet connects wirelessly to another radio, which you know as a router, but may also be called an "access point".

WiFi Frequency Bands and Channels

WiFi supports two radio frequencies: 2.4GHz and 5GHz. This is analogous to the AM and FM bands on most car radios. Just as there are different stations or "channels" on AM and FM radios, the 2.4GHz band of WiFi has several channels available for use as well, numbered 1 through 11. For the purposes of home use, we use only the channels 1, 6, and 11 because they do not interfere with each other. Importantly, the 5GHz band has many more channels available for use, but this is not the only difference.

Just as you can't have two different radio stations broadcasting on the same channel or too close together on the radio dial, similar issues can affect your WiFi. All routers should be tuned to one of the three available 2.4 GHz WiFi channels, and if your neighbor is using the same channel on her router as you are, you'll both have performance issues. Luckily, you can *change* the channel! (I'll tell you how later.)

Virtually every smartphone, tablet, Mac, and PC will support both the 2.4 and 5GHz frequency bands. Other types of devices that connect to WiFi may not support 5GHz. Your home network will be set up to use both, just like having an AM/FM radio.

You may have noticed in your car that AM radio stations typically keep playing much further away from where the signal originates than FM stations do. This is a function of the way that radio waves pass through different objects and materials (like dirt, concrete, and air, for instance). In technical terms, we call this "propagation characteristics". In general, lower frequencies travel further and through more solid objects than higher frequencies.

The lower frequency of the WiFi 2.4GHz band will cover the average sized home, penetrating most walls and ceilings and will often leak out onto the street and into neighbors' homes. (Certainly, in an apartment complex it's not uncommon to have a list of several dozen available networks in the 2.4GHz band). The higher frequency 5GHz radio band channels do not penetrate walls as well as the 2.4GHz channels do, and generally speaking you're likely to have more dead spots using the 5GHz band. But: the 5GHz band comes with the significant advantage of having dozens of non-interfering channels available for use, meaning that if you can get decent coverage at 5GHz in your home, it's advantageous to use it.

WiFi Network Name or SSID

There is one more important concept to understand about WiFi that is called the SSID, (Service Set Identifier) also known as the WiFi Network Name. This is important because the SSID is the name of the WiFi network that you see on your smartphone or computer when you connect to WiFi. An SSID can represent either a 2.4GHz frequency channel or a 5GHz frequency channel or both (meaning a single SSID can represent both 2.4 and 5GHz WiFi networks at the same time, but we won't be doing it this way). Later in the router chapter, I'll cover how to set these up and how to name them optimally so that connecting new Smart Home devices is simple.

Encryption

Encryption means that all of the data that you send and receive from your computer or Smart Home device to the Router using WiFi is jumbled in such a way that nobody (within reason) can snoop in on it. The best and most easily configured encryption type is called "WPA2 Personal". You'll have to remember a password, but that is a small price to pay for reasonable security. On your smartphone or computer, when you see a little lock icon next to a WiFi network you want to join, it means that the network is encrypted and you will need a password to join in. This is in contrast to many public WiFi networks at hotels and hotspots that do not have the lock but offer a temporary login page that asks for a

This is a long and complicated subject but the only thing you really need to know is that all of your data — uploaded and downloaded — should be encrypted when using WiFi.

password. In this case you are not on an encrypted link and some people call this type of connection a hacker's delight.

Now, that wasn't so bad, was it? Feel free to refer back to these terms as you read on. Now it is time to set up your router.

Chapter 2 – Setting Up Your Router

The thought of getting a router might already be giving you the shivers, but not to worry - just carefully follow the steps and you'll be up and running in no time.

By now, you have selected your Internet service provider and told them that you want to install your own router and WiFi, and the segment of the network we are working on here is the network inside your home. Designing this with Smart Home in mind, there is one big difference in the way you'll approach this task from what you used to do when you just stuck the router provided by your ISP in a corner and turned it on. In the past, if there was a place in your home that didn't have WiFi connectivity (a dead spot), you just moved around until you got better signal, since it only meant moving your laptop or phone.

With a Smart Home, a new approach is needed. Once you install a light switch, door lock, thermostat, video doorbell, sprinkler controller, window shade, and so on, those devices aren't going to be moved. For a Smart Home, your network wireless signal must cover the whole house and be strong enough everywhere you want to install a Smart Home device. You also have to be able to easily measure this before you go out and buy something so you know up front it's going to work. As mentioned earlier, there are two WiFi networks (2.4GHz and 5GHz) and you will need to set up both. This is not as difficult as it may sound, but this chapter will go into some detail just to make sure everything is done correctly.

What kind of router should you buy? If you go into the store or online, there seems to be a limitless choice of products from the likes of Netgear, Belkin, Linksys, Apple, and others. Having worked in this industry and spending time at Linksys and being loyal to that brand while I worked at Cisco (who used to own Linksys), I can honestly tell you that you can pick any of these and get them to work for *basic* connectivity. It might not be fun to sort through all the jargon on the boxes and the techno-talk that many of the sales people in the stores will send your way, though.

Several years ago, I broke from my tradition of buying the brand of the company I worked for and I am glad I did. In about 2008, I made the strategic decision to move from the world of PC's to the world of Apple, starting with my laptop and then later iPhones and Apple TV. I will go into the reasons for that later on (hint: simplicity and a MUCH more stable environment) but at the same time I took a chance and bought an Apple Airport Extreme Router for my home networking (about US $200 on the Apple Store).

This by far, has been the most stable, simplest WiFi router I have ever used and I have not had to reboot it a single time in the many years since I got it. It may seem kind of expensive, but whether or not you have any other Apple products, this is still what I would buy. It also has the added advantage of being able to centralize the ultrasimple computer backups that we should all be doing, which I will go into detail later on.

Importantly, a *single* router in your home may or may not get you the coverage you need for both 2.4GHz and 5GHz in all the locations you can anticipate installing a Smart Home device. It is therefore critical to have a plan on what to do if you need to extend that network. In almost all cases, that requires adding another router or two to broaden the WiFi range and get rid of dead spots. In the case of Apple, another Airport Extreme or the lesser expensive Airport Express (about US $100) performs that function, wirelessly connecting (or with Ethernet if you happen to have home wiring) to the main router and extending both WiFi networks to further flung regions of the home.

In fact, there are quite a number of new home wireless systems becoming available from both established vendors and startups that perform this so called "mesh WiFi". Since this is a new area that is changing so rapidly, I've made an overview of these possibilities available online at www.smarthomeprofessor.com/wifi. The example in this chapter will use the Apple router products, but all the same settings and principles apply to any of the alternatives.

From a home router WiFi perspective, these are the main requirements I would strongly recommend and why.

Feature or Function	Why?
Dual band simultaneous 2.4GHz and 5GHz radios with the ability to assign different SSIDs to each network	You will need them both for optimal performance especially as more and more devices get connected
Gigabit Ethernet (1000Mbps) WAN (Wide Area Network) port	You probably don't need it yet but Internet speeds are increasing so be prepared
Several Gigabit Ethernet LAN (Local Area Network) ports – four is ideal	If you want to plug other stuff in that is near the router (and you will), this comes in handy
No ugly antennas sticking out	They will break, they are ugly and there is no need for them to be external anymore
A single light that will tell you if all is well	Simple is better and there is a better chance for optimal placement in your home
An Ultra simple way of configuring, typically done with a phone App and/or computer app	Otherwise you will get mad at me for telling you to buy your own router
Optional – A USB port that supports a shared storage drive	Very handy when doing centralized backups for multiple computers

I won't provide detailed installation guides for all possible scenarios but I'll show you how my setup works and yours will likely be similar.

Physically, this is how a router (left) connects to a modem (right) that in turn plugs into the cable or phone outlet. Cable and DSL Modems are about US $50-$70 and can be bought at any electronics store. It

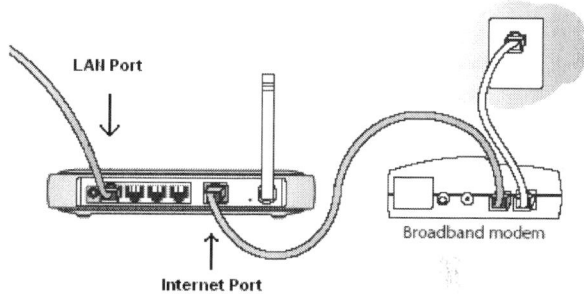

LAH Port

Internet Port

Broadband modem

doesn't really matter what brand you buy, but make sure it is compatible with your Internet service. There is no configuration required on most modems so just plug it in and it is all set to go. The router shown on the left of the diagram plugs into the modem using the included Ethernet cable. From there, you may have some devices plugged into the router but the vast majority of devices will connect wirelessly using WiFi.

Some ISPs insist that you use their modem and router combination. If you are stuck with this, I would still get your own router and plug it in through the one supplied by the ISP. If you do this, turn off all the WiFi settings on the ISP router.

The devices supplied by your ISP are often combinations of modem and router all in one. This might seem attractive at first but the downside is that they usually rent them to you for upwards of $10/month and there is not much control to configure things the way you will need to for proper Smart Home coverage.

Below is a picture of my network from the Apple Airport setup utility. It shows the main Airport Extreme plugged into the Internet connection (it doesn't show the modem). When setting up the router, there

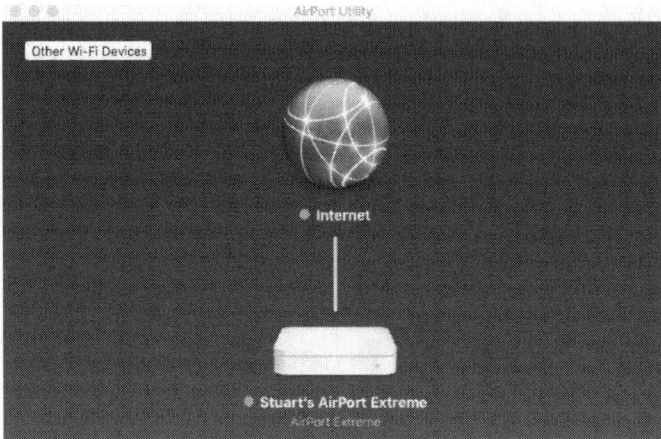

aren't too many things that you need to worry about but you will want to get them right. I'll illustrate how the Apple Router is set up and which settings are important and which are optional and you can apply these same principles to whichever product you choose.

The first thing to do is decide physically where to put the main router. The first choice is that it be near either a coaxial cable outlet for cable service, or a phone jack for DSL. Often you will have multiple locations available so you should try to pick the one that is most centrally located in the home so you get the best WiFi coverage possible. Depending upon the size of your home, you may need to extend your wireless coverage by using another router, a set-up I explain in a few pages. In general, it is worth trying to see if you get good enough coverage with just one router and then only add more if you need them. This is somewhat counter to the marketing strategies of the new wave of WiFi mesh networking vendors who like to sell you two or three routers at a time, insisting that you will need them all. It will certainly work, but you may be paying way too much by not trying a single router first.

Router setup

We'll continue to use the example of an Apple Airport Extreme router. All configuration is done using the Airport Utility program that is included on every Mac, iPhone, and iPad and is also downloadable for a Windows PC. Each of the major settings will be shown with a screenshot and explained what they should be set to and why.

Base Station – Router name and password

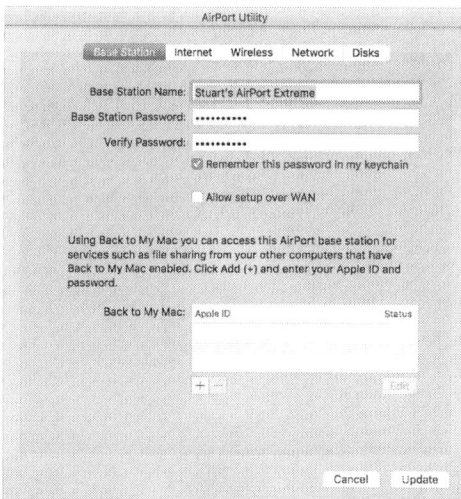

Pick anything for the name but pick a good password and when prompted to remember the password in Keychain, accept. (I'll talk more about Mac's Keychain function when I discuss System

33

Preferences in Chapter 3) This password is for changing settings on your router. Do *not* give this out to anyone. It is *not* the password that you use to get on the wireless network from your phone or computer. That comes later.

Internet setting

Check with your Internet provider but usually choose DHCP if you have Cable and PPPoE if you are using DSL. This is how the Internet side of your network will know about your router. The Router address (blacked out) and other things in grey should automatically fill in. You don't need to change anything in the "Internet Options..." button on the bottom.

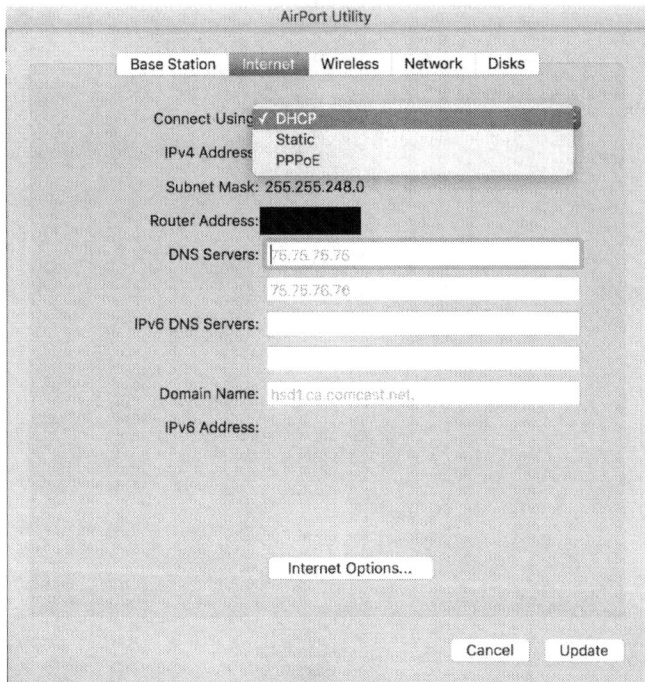

Wireless Setup

This is the tab where you create your main 2.4GHz WiFi network and, optionally, a guest network for guests and visitors. Pick a wireless network name (aka SSID) that you will be able to identify as your network. Your neighbors will see it too, so use clean language. In this example, if my name is Smith, I might pick smith2 to denote my 2.4GHz network and smithguest for a guest network. In both cases, choose WPA2 Personal for network security. The main wireless password will be used by you and your family, so pick something you can remember but *not* the same password as the router or ones you use for other purposes online or on your personal hard drives. The guest network password should be different yet again, and you can post this password on the fridge for guests to see. Also, click the box to save the password in your keychain.

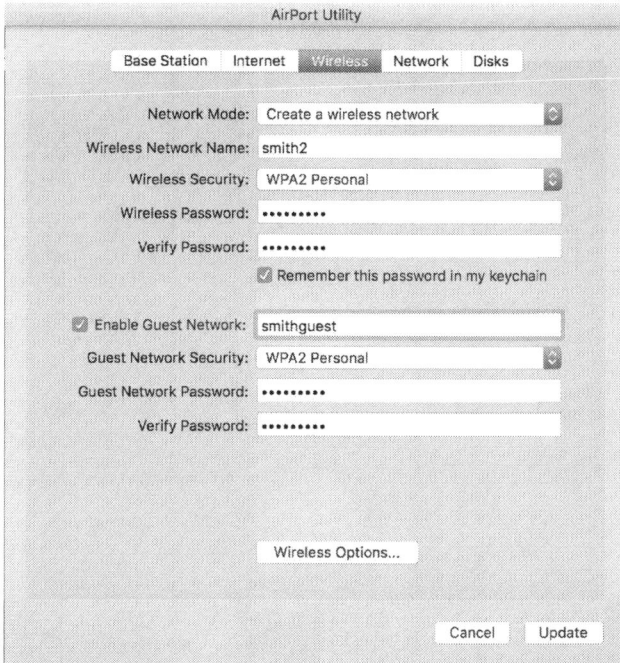

Wireless options

Apple puts the 5GHz WiFi network configuration under this tab. Set it up as shown in the illustration and pick a different network name than you gave your 2.4GHz network. This will be important later when you want to test to see whether you have enough signal strength and you have to test a specific network. If the names are the same, then you won't know which network you are testing, the 2.4GHz or 5GHz, and many devices only connect to the 2.4 GHz network. Some of the newer WiFi mesh products don't allow you to have different network names in their effort to simplify things, but I think this is a mistake and hopefully they will add this level of flexibility down the road. *Do not* check the 'create hidden network' box, and set both of the radio channels to "Automatic". You may or may not see the radio mode selection. If you do, it gets a bit nerdy but it turns out there are many variants of both 2.4GHz and 5GHz WiFi

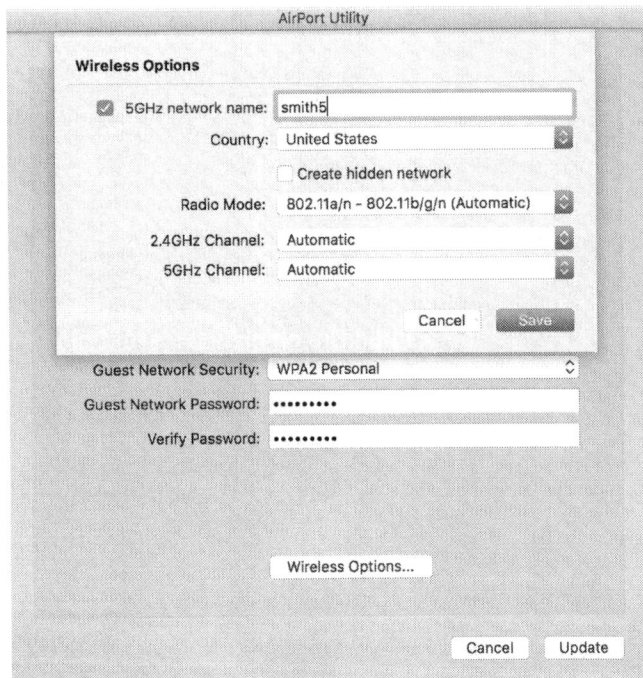

networking so you always want to pick the latest one that is available which is usually at the top of the list. OK, enough of that! Don't give up yet. You're almost done!

Get your geek on!

The term 802.11a refers to the 5GHz network and if you have the latest access point or router it will probably say 802.11a/n/ac.

The 802.11b/g/n network is the 2.4GHz network.

Network

On the main router, use a router mode of "DHCP and NAT". The DHCP range is the range of addresses that will be assigned to the devices on your network. In general, you would leave this at their default values for the router

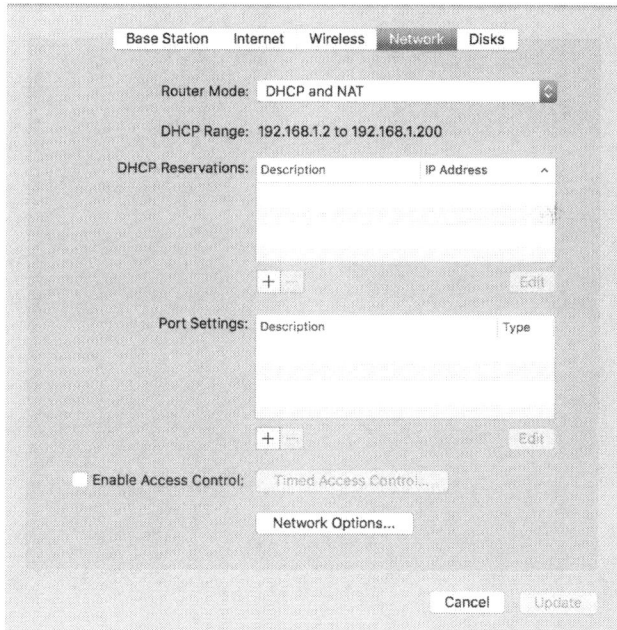

| Base Station | Internet | Wireless | Network | Disks |

Router Mode: DHCP and NAT

DHCP Range: 192.168.1.2 to 192.168.1.200

DHCP Reservations: Description   IP Address

+ —   Edit

Port Settings: Description   Type

+ —   Edit

Enable Access Control: Timed Access Control...

Network Options...

Cancel   Update

which would allow for over 250 connected devices on your network. I changed mine by clicking on the Network options button, but you won't need to do that.

Disks

This is a setting specific to the Apple Airport Extreme router and requires a third-party USB disk drive to be plugged in to the USB port on the router. This is most useful as your one disk to backup all your computers. There is more detail on this in the Backup section in the next chapter on Computers but this is the main reason that I am sticking with the Apple router products until I can find another vendor who has this extremely valuable feature. The name of the disk will likely be different than what I have here but any name is fine. Make sure you click

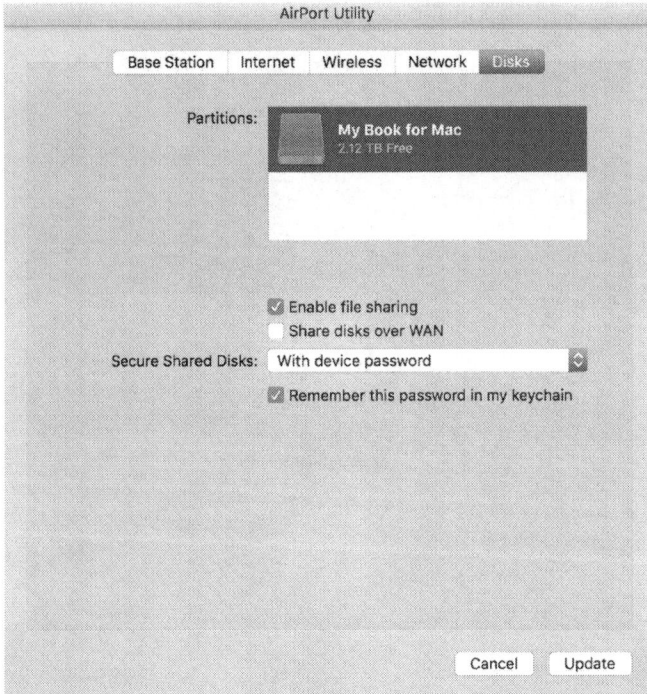

on the update button when you are complete. The router will reset itself and you will temporarily disconnect, but when the green light comes back on solid, reconnect to one of the new WiFi networks you just created and you are done with the main router.

Extending your WiFi range

In a later section, you'll learn how to easily test whether or not you have WiFi dead spots in your house, and if you discover some, remember to come back to this section so you can learn how to set up an Airport Express (cheaper and smaller than the main Airport Extreme, but you can still use the Extreme as an extender) as a wireless extender off the main router. This diagram, courtesy of the Apple support

site, shows the main Airport Extreme router in the middle and the new Airport Express on the right. The key to success is the physical placement of the Express router so that it is within wireless range of the main router but extends that WiFi range to areas of poor coverage. All you need is an AC plug in the wall and a place to put the tiny Express router.

The configuration of this extender router is trivial because all of this gets filled in for you if you ask it to simply extend your wireless network. Follow the directions that come with the router and choose "Extend a wireless network". All of the same settings that you had on the main router automatically get carried over to the new router configured as a network extender.

In my case, I was having difficulty getting enough wireless signal to a video doorbell (video requires higher data throughput than other devices) so I ended up using Velcro to attach the extension router out of sight and inside the bottom of a grandfather clock. The newer generation of WiFi mesh routers (discussed on www.smarthomeprofessor.com/wifi) also make configuration of the second and third routers simple, by taking the settings of the main unit and using the appropriate network names and passwords so that you can't make a mistake. Some models, however, don't allow different network names for the 2.4GHz and 5GHz networks and as of mid-2017, none of them allow you to plug in a USB drive to do centralized backups.

That's it for setting up your WiFi networks. There may be some adjustments later as you start to test out specific spots for wireless signal strength, but this is a good starting point and a thorough foundation for your Smart Home. Remember that later on, if you do find dead spots, you can physically move routers to different locations or add another router off of the main unit just like we did with this one. After doing this with an AirPort Express, the network looks like this: The dotted line between the 2 routers indicates a

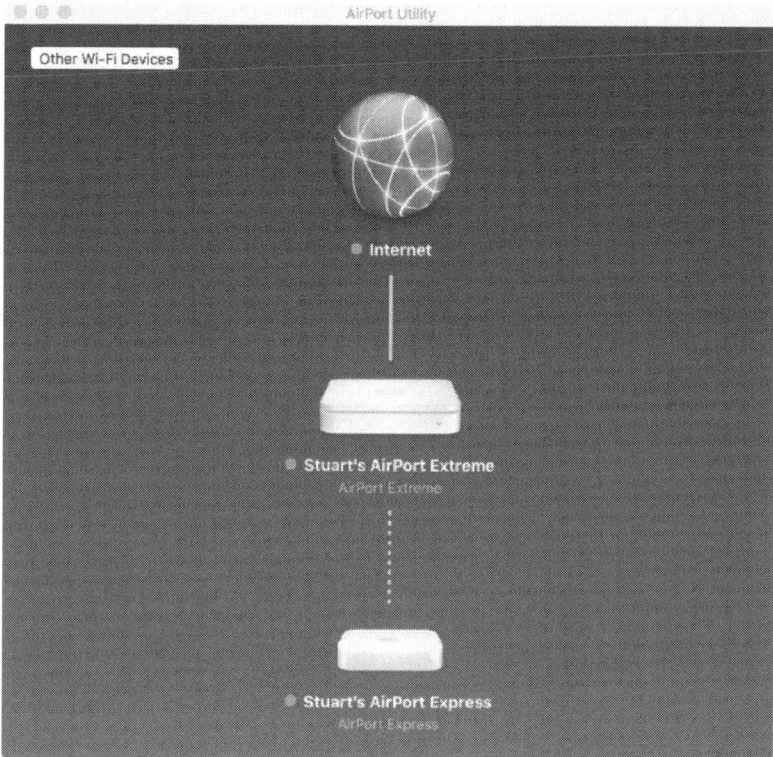

wireless connection. If your home happens to be wired with Ethernet wiring, use it to connect the 2 routers and you will get better performance.

Chapter 3 – Computers and Smartphones

Your new digital, automated lifestyle can be run from any number of devices, and most likely you'll be operating it from your smartphone. You can also operate your Smart Home from your computer, PC, tablet, and with some products, your watch, too. Since almost everyone has a laptop or desktop computer, I'll start with that set-up first.

I was once a dedicated PC guy, but after the iPhone came out in the mid-2000s, I started a gradual switch to Apple products. Your preference is personal, of course, but my reasons for switching to Apple were that they were developing a leading-edge product line that already had consistent technical design, similarity in use between Apple products and overall stability compared to the PC environment. The ease-of-use with Apple is reason alone to switch, but whether you're Mac or PC, the same principles apply to using your computer to operate your Smart Home.

The minimum amount of memory (as of late 2017) I would put in a Mac is eight Gigabytes. If you can upgrade it inexpensively, it's probably the place I would put any extra money. The amount of disk storage and the type of drive is directly a function of the kinds of things you will be doing. If you expect to take a lot of pictures or videos, you will want more storage. Generally, starting with 250 Gigabytes is the minimum and the less moving parts the better, so a solid-state drive (while more expensive) is a bit more robust, faster and longer lasting for a laptop. I recently bought Apple MacBooks on sale in their default configuration (eight Gigabytes of memory and 250 Gigabytes of solid state hard drive) and have been quite happy with them on price and performance. For my desktop iMac, I have 1 Terabyte of disk and that is the main repository of my photos and videos.

Important settings for your Mac

All of the system settings on a Mac can be found in System Preferences, which you will find under the Apple menu in the upper left-hand corner of the screen.

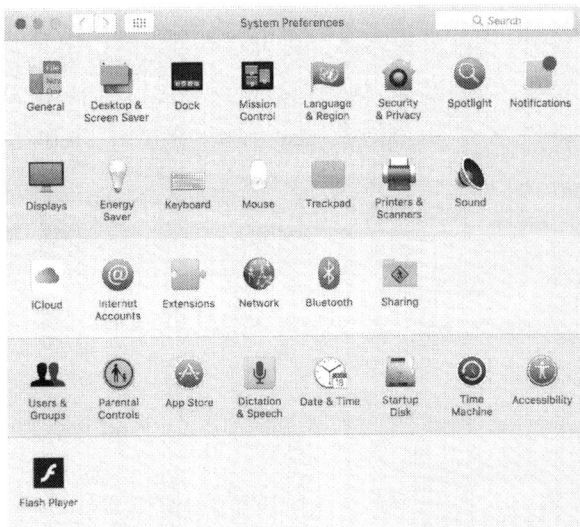

Start with the General Tab in Security and Privacy. Make sure that you have a login password set for your computer. This is the password that unlocks the computer when you open the lid and start to use it. Remember it and don't give it to anyone else. I have my computer set to sleep at one minute and I have to re-enter my password again after that. I recommend you keep your sleep time at one minute or less for security reasons.

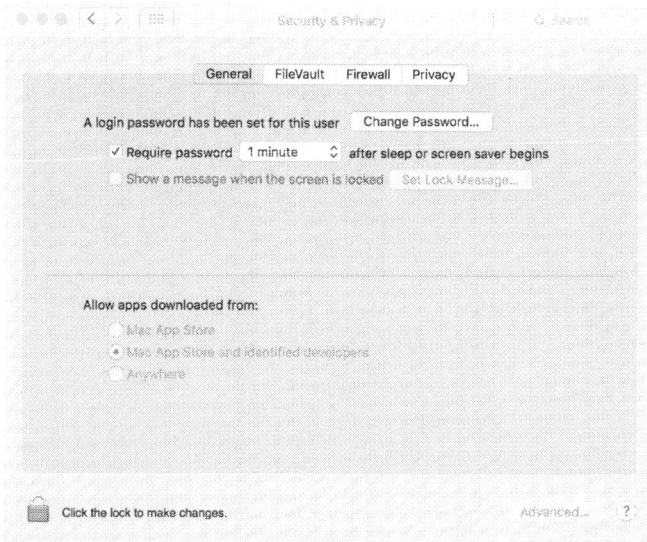

Select the FileVault tab so that all your files are encrypted on your computer. You won't notice any difference in performance but if your machine is stolen,

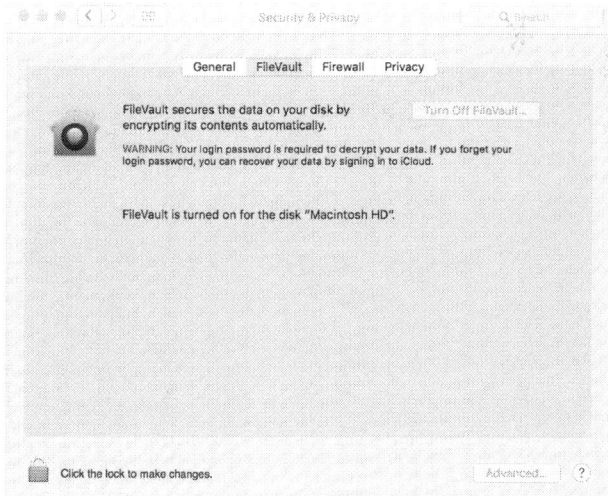

nobody will be able to get the files off of your machine, even if they remove the hard drive.

Turn your computer's firewall on. It makes it harder for hackers to access your computer and again, only in rare occasions will you notice anything different.

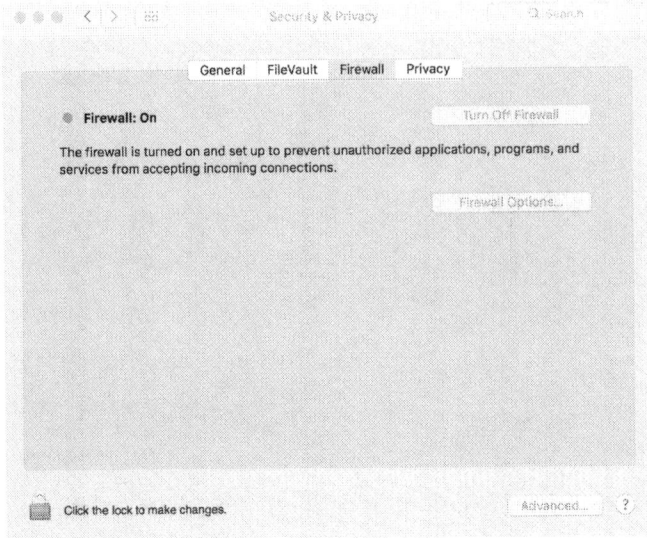

The Trackpad setting is not *that* important but if your Mac has one, spend some time learning the different finger movements that are so eloquently illustrated when you choose the Trackpad setting in System Preferences. It can save you lots of time as you get better using

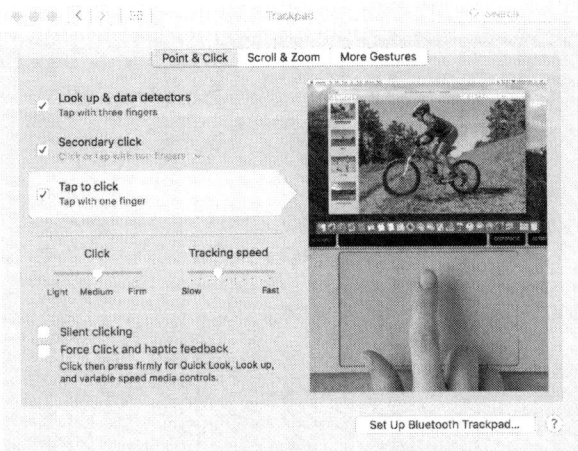

the machine. If you don't like a change you made, you can just change it back.

iCloud settings are very important and will make life so simple, especially when you have more than one Apple device of any kind. The "cloud" is not actually a collection of ice crystals thirty thousand feet in the air somehow keeping your files safe (and cold!). There are many clouds and they're all data centers. They're designed not just for extra security and back-up but so you can access whatever's in it across all of your registered Apple devices. If you don't have an Apple ID, you can create one easily. You can do it on your iPhone or iPad by tapping "iCloud" in Settings and then clicking on "Create a new Apple ID." To do this on your computer, go to apple.com and search "Apple ID" for easy instructions.

Your Apple ID password is another one of the important ones that you need to remember as you will use this to link all your Apple devices in iCloud. Check all of the boxes as shown on the screenshot above and click on the options button for photos and set it as shown. I don't usually click on the first one because I have a huge photo library that would take days to upload but feel free to use this if you want. Keep in mind that

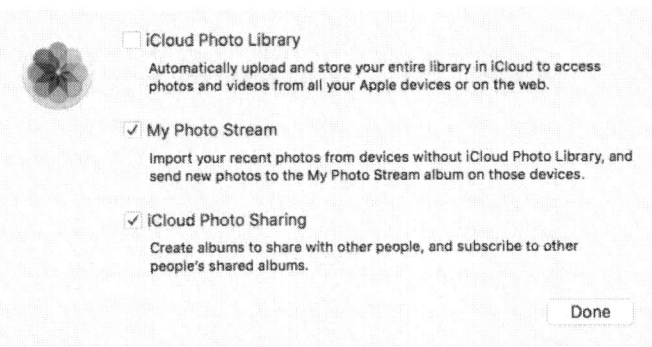

iCloud Photo Library
Automatically upload and store your entire library in iCloud to access photos and videos from all your Apple devices or on the web.

✓ My Photo Stream
Import your recent photos from devices without iCloud Photo Library, and send new photos to the My Photo Stream album on those devices.

✓ iCloud Photo Sharing
Create albums to share with other people, and subscribe to other people's shared albums.

Done

you get 5GB of free storage with your iCloud account and then you can upgrade to something larger if you have a photo library bigger than 5GB (approximately 1000-1500 photos taken with an iPhone). The cost to upgrade to 50GB is currently only 99¢ a month.

Scroll down to the bottom of the iCloud settings to find the Keychain. The keychain is where passwords are stored for anything done on your computer including most applications and most web browsing. When you are prompted to save a password in the Keychain you should always do so (unless the password didn't work!)

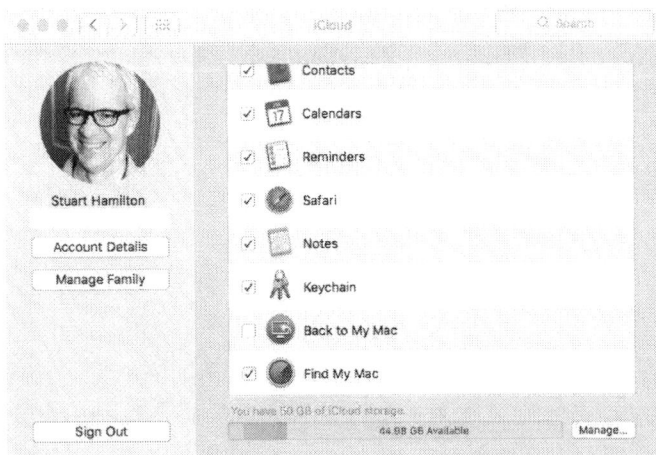

Stuart Hamilton

Account Details

Manage Family

Sign Out

iCloud

✓ Contacts
✓ Calendars
✓ Reminders
✓ Safari
✓ Notes
✓ Keychain
☐ Back to My Mac
✓ Find My Mac

You have 50 GB of iCloud storage.
44.98 GB Available   Manage...

Keychain also securely stores all of your passwords in iCloud. Once you pick a password on one Apple device, it is automatically recalled on all your other devices. So, if you log into a website on your computer using a password and it was saved in the Keychain, you can use your iPhone or iPad to log into the same site without remembering that password.

The Apple app Store is where you will get most of your programs that you run on the Mac. Every time you install a program it leaves you with the burden of having to update it on a regular basis. It can be annoying to get interrupted constantly about upgrades so I check the boxes as shown so that it happens automatically. I was afraid to do this at first because I was worried about downloading a bad update and wrecking something, but my experience on the Mac has been very positive with updates, so unless you were to research each one in detail before updating, it really makes a lot of sense to let the computer do the work so that you can focus on doing more useful things.

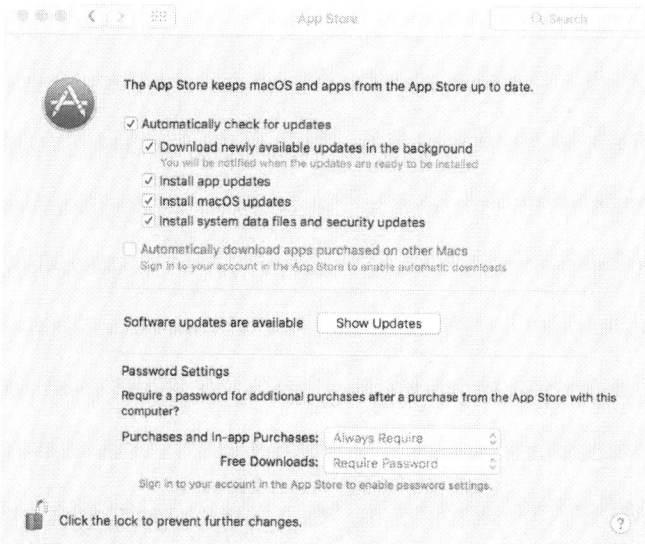

The final set-up is for Time Machine, Apple's backup system. When I had a PC, I never did backups because it

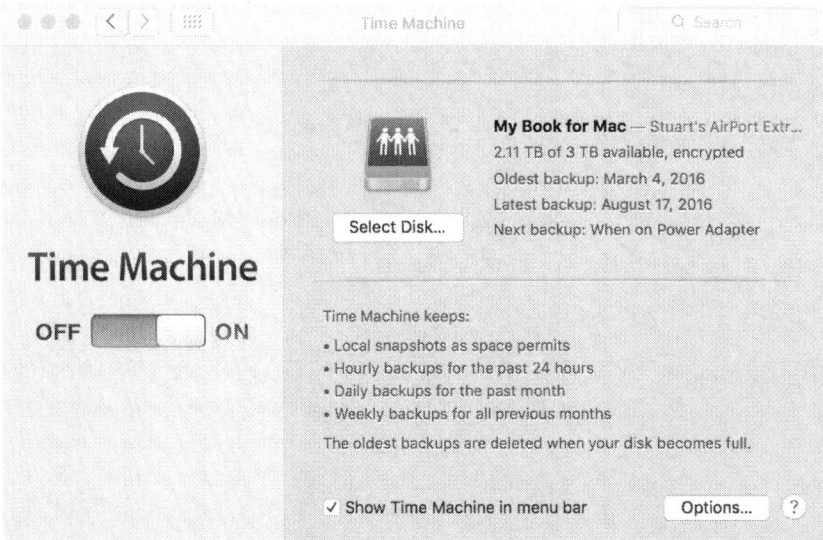

was too hard and it slowed my machine down to a snail's pace. With Time Machine, it's extremely easy and it also works! If something goes wrong with your Mac or if it's stolen or lost, you can restore it to the exact state it was in, or to any date since Time Machine was installed. Also, it's so important to encrypt your backups so that nobody can ever steal your backup hard drive and get the files. Again, this backup encryption will require a password that you have to remember.

There are a couple of hardware options for backing up your Mac. You can buy individual USB disks (at virtually any electronics store) for each of your Macs and plug them in and run Time Machine. I used to do this, but I simplified things recently when I bought one larger drive and plugged it into the USB port of the Airport Extreme router I mentioned earlier in the book. By centralizing the backup drive, I use it to back up all of the Macs that we have in the house.

Remember the lesson on WiFi, where I talked about having separate 2.4GHz and 5GHz networks? When you do backups with the centralized backup disk drive on the Airport Extreme router, you are using the wireless network to get the data to the router so you want the fastest possible transmission which most frequently happens on the 5GHz network. So, I normally run all the Mac computers in the house on the 5GHz network largely for that reason but also because there are many older devices that only run on the 2.4GHz network and I don't want computer backups to interfere with those devices.

Adding Smartphones and Tablets

Once again, there are only two viable choices in the smartphone world, Apple iPhones or Android phones. In the Apple world, there are new iPhone models every year to choose from but from a software perspective, Apple is in control of the software and updates. It is pretty normal in the iPhone world to keep your phone and apps automatically and regularly updated. In the Android world, updates are usually done through your carrier so over time the number of versions of software floating around in Android phones can become rather large. Application developers find it easier to build and test their applications in the iPhone world since it is a more homogeneous environment.

This is important when choosing Smart Home products and looking at reviews. It is fairly common for the Android version of an app to arrive after the iPhone version and the quality of the Android version may take a while to catch up, too. I've used both, but choose to use an iPhone for its simplicity and also because many functions get better when you are using all Apple products, as you'll see later. The examples I use will be for the iPhone but similar principles apply for Android.

Choosing a Wireless Carrier

Carrier plans are ever changing and expensive, so it pays to shop around at least once a year to make sure you're getting the best deal. Always start with evaluating the cellular coverage in the areas you mainly use your phone. On an iPhone, look on the top left of your phone at the number of dots or bars you have. This is an indication of the strength of the voice network for making voice calls. Now turn WiFi off temporarily. You should always see LTE right after the dots/bars on the top left of the phone screen. LTE is the latest high-speed data network, faster than 4G, 3G, Edge or any other that you might see. Make sure you can get LTE data in the areas you use the phone most. If you are thinking of switching, look at the coverage on other people's phones with other carrier networks before switching to another provider.

For the most part, in the US, all local, long distance calling and texting are included in your plan along with a certain amount of data. But how much data do you need? 2GB per month is almost the minimum now with some plans in the 4-6GB per month and many are now unlimited. None of the data you use while on WiFi counts towards this limit (although, when you are at home it does count towards your home Internet data limits, if you have them). The main thing to look for on the data plan is that you don't get an overage charge if you use more than your allotment. Also watch for international data roaming charges that can literally add hundreds if not thousands of dollars to your monthly bill if you are not careful - one of the huge rip-offs the cellular companies have enjoyed for years that thankfully is starting to be replaced by all-inclusive plans and travel packages, some of which load automatically when you leave the country.

After that, it boils down to cost, so shop around. When the iPhone 7 came out, there was a period of 2-3 weeks where I could upgrade my two-year-old iPhone 6 for free, but you have to jump on these quickly to take advantage of the savings. Also, if you have a family plan with more than two devices, there are often pretty good deals, especially for the third phone and beyond.

There are a number of key settings on the iPhone that you will want to make life easier and facilitate an easy Smart Home experience. I will cover the important ones here.

iCloud Settings

Some of the most useful features of the iPhone are enabled when you use iCloud similar to the example shown earlier for the Mac computer. (On iPhone, go to Settings and iCloud). Use your Apple ID and password to log into iCloud and I would recommend that you set all the of the functions in the iCloud settings to "on". Among other things, you will be able to get pictures taken on your iPhone onto other devices like your computers, AppleTV, or tablet, and easily share them with others. Phone backups to iCloud happen automatically when your phone is plugged in and is on WiFi. All your passwords that you use on your Mac computer are now automatically filled in on the phone when using Safari as a browser so you don't have to remember them. Files stored in your iCloud drive are there and available on the phone. These are just a few of the reasons that you'll want to do this and there are many more that you will discover.

WiFi Settings

It is important that you can connect to both your 2.4GHz and 5GHz home networks from your phone, so make sure you can use them both and know how to switch between them using the settings button and then WiFi. Even though they need a password, if you have it stored in your iCloud keychain you won't have to enter it. If you do have to enter the password for the first time, you will only need to do it once.

Your phone will be the primary measurement device to help you figure out whether a new Smart Home device is going to work or not at a specific location. It will also determine if you need to extend your WiFi network to far flung areas of your home. If somewhere in your home, your 5GHz WiFi network is not showing up on your phone, move within sight of the main router and try it again since 5GHz WiFi networks won't have as far a reach as their 2.4GHz equivalents.

Password and Touch ID

You absolutely MUST have a password on your phone. You can use only numbers or a regular alphanumeric keyboard to create a password. Remember this password and don't use it on your other devices. I would also highly recommend enabling Touch ID so you can use your fingerprint to log onto your phone and even some apps, which is very handy. Even though this has nothing to do with Smart Home, you can also use it for Apple Pay which you will love once you start to use it. In the future, Apple may come up with more advanced techniques to uniquely identify you, so keep an eye on this and use fingerprint technology if it's available to you.

Voice Control – Siri

Siri allows you to talk to your phone and give it commands which will be used later when controlling your Smart Home devices (e.g. "Hey Siri, turn on the kitchen lights"). It's trained to your voice so, unlike some other voice recognition devices, when I ask Siri to do something in the presence of several iPhones, only mine will be triggered. Go to Settings and Siri on your iPhone to turn this on and follow the directions.

These are the main functions you'll use regularly on your iPhone along with apps that you will need to control the Smart Home devices you will be installing in your home. It is probably a good idea to also enable automatic app updates, since keeping all these up to date is not something to spend your precious time doing manually.

The next chapter will show you how to measure your network performance using your computer and smartphone. You will see from my results what kind of a difference in speed can result from the two different WiFi networks.

Chapter 4 – Measuring the Network

At this point you have your own router programmed for two wireless networks (2.4GHz and 5GHz), each with their own network name; you have a computer and smartphone that are each wirelessly connected to the router with Internet access working. Now, you want to find out if your network is working up to snuff! Let's do that.

1) Situate yourself within sight of your router so that you get the best possible wireless signal.

2) Using your computer or smartphone, connect yourself to the WiFi network that corresponds to your 5GHz wireless network.

3) Open a browser on your computer and go the web site www.speedtest.net. On your phone, download and use the "Speedtest by Ookla" app.

Ignore all the ads all over the page and hit the "run test" button.

The first thing measured is the delay between you and the test site. This is shown under PING and it should be well under 100ms (100 milliseconds) typically. Next, the

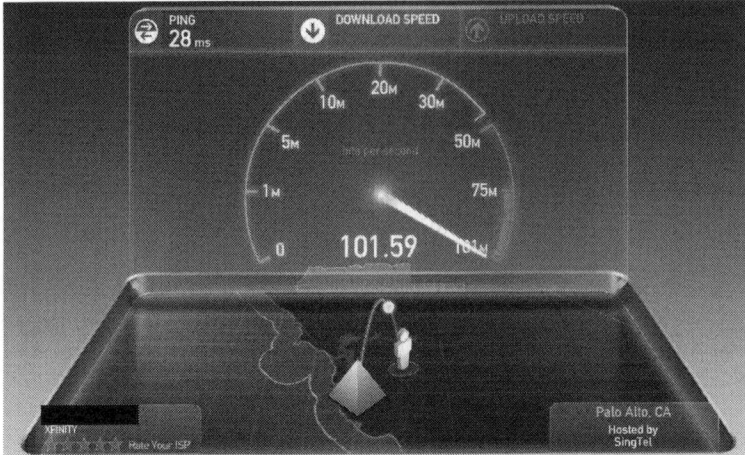

download speed is measured (data coming from the network to you) and in this case, we are cruising along at 101.59 Mbps (Megabits per second) which is pretty good since I signed up for a 75Mbps service.

After the final download speed is determined, it does an upload speed test followed by the final results.

Ignoring all the nonsense at the bottom, my final results for the 5GHz wireless network, through the router and to the test point in the Internet were: 102.59Mbps Down and 6.17Mbps Up. As mentioned earlier, it might seem odd that

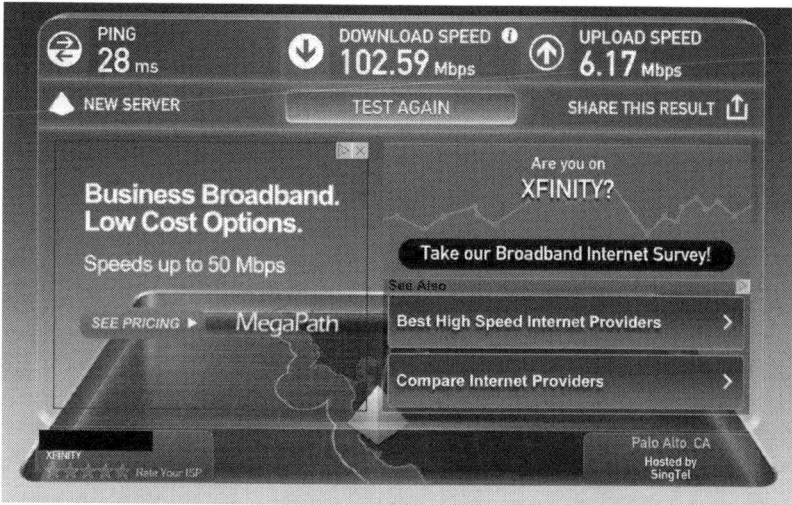

there is such a difference in the service speeds but it is quite normal to have this type of mismatch as most often you are pulling in data from the network. However, if you choose to do massive backups from your computers to the Cloud (like Apple iCloud, Google Drive, Box, Dropbox, etc.) then having a faster upload speed will make a measurable improvement. The only way to do this is to pick an Internet plan that offers the speeds you desire.

When I switch to my 2.4GHz network (the one that is typically busier and more utilized by neighbor's interfering networks), the speedtest results are quite different.

The download speed dropped from 102.59Mbps to 65.67Mbps. Why? When you do these tests, you are

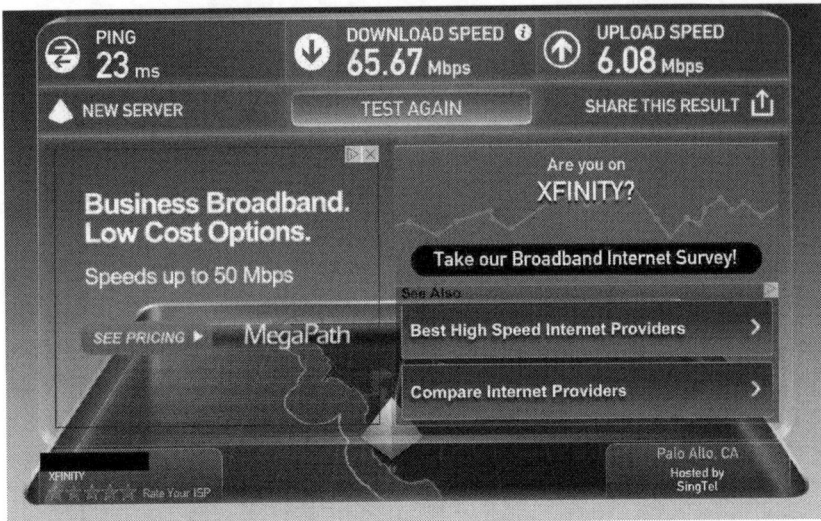

measuring the speed from the test point on the Internet, through the Internet, from the ISP to your home, and back to your computer over WiFi. The maximum speed you get is determined by the weakest link in the chain. In this example, the upload speeds are virtually the same because the weakest upload link is my Internet provider who throttles my service at 6Mbps. So, in my case, both wireless networks inside the home are faster than that, so the 6Mbps choke point is indicative of the segment between my home and the Internet Provider being the slowest part of the path for uploads.

The download speed is different though. What we can see here is that on the 2.4GHz wireless network, the choke point is my wireless network inside the home, between the router and my computer/smartphone, since we know that the rest of the path can achieve at least 102Mbps, as seen on the 5GHz network.

If you didn't follow all of that, it's okay. What you need to know is that the 2.4GHz wireless network is only about 60% as fast as the 5GHz network in my house. In my case, part of the reason for the slower 2.4GHz connection is the number of strong network signals coming from nearby homes that interfere with my network. Remember, the 2.4GHz network only has 3 channels that should be used (1, 6, or 11) which don't interfere with one another. Also, some people like to think they are clever by deciding to use a channel number like 3 or 4 but all that does is interfere with both channel 1 and 6 at the same time. There is not much you can do about this except to create a good 5GHz network that has broad coverage in your home.

Doing this test will be a normal task when deciding to install a new Smart Home device, and it's best to do it with your smartphone. Download the speedtest app for your smartphone and get good at doing this test from various points on both 2.4GHz and 5GHz networks.

Your results will vary from mine and will even vary at different times of the day as networks are being used by other people both in your home and your neighbor's. But it's good to get a handle on how your system normally performs to compare it to performance levels when you have a problem with speed.

Chapter 5 – Security and Passwords

If you were around before the Internet became a thing in the mid 1990's, you probably remember doing things like mailing paper checks. If someone decided to steal your letter with the check in it, they would have your full name, address, phone number, bank account number and signature. With that information of course, you could be vulnerable to all kinds of fraud and theft, but thankfully banks would reimburse you if funds were stolen through no fault of your own.

Nowadays, with most transactions happening electronically, we are also at risk of fraud and theft, and to minimize that risk, there are some important steps that we must take in our electronic lives to do our best to prevent these things from happening. Some techniques are peppered throughout the book like encrypting your hard drives, doing encrypted backups, encrypting and password protecting your WiFi network and others. This chapter focuses mostly on passwords, your multiple points of entry into your digital world which encompass e-mail, social media, banking, Smart Home, bill paying, investments, and just about everything you do with your phone or computer.

It is almost an annual occurrence with me now that there is a fraudulent charge on a credit card and I have to get a replacement card. It likely will happen to you too, so while we do everything to minimize risk, we also have to realize that bad things happen and we have to be prepared for how to deal with them. Thinking of glossing over this chapter? Take a deep breath and read on. It will be worth it.

You will have hundreds of passwords over time, and as tempting as it is to use the same password for all your logins, *don't do it.* We obviously can't remember that many unique complex passwords though, so there must be a better way. It turns out that there are a small handful of passwords that you will have to remember but with the use of a password manager (like iCloud Keychain), you don't have to know any of the other ones, although you'll be able to look them up if you need to.

These are the passwords that you have to remember and they should all be different:

- Computer password(s)
- Smartphone password
- Apple ID password
- FileVault Encryption password

- WiFi passwords are handy to remember but not absolutely necessary - remember the 2.4GHz and 5GHz passwords should be the same, but different from your guest network password

The passwords above should be ones that contain uppercase and lowercase letters, numbers, and special characters in some form that is not easily guessed. You just have to do this and remember them. So far, that isn't too bad, but what about the rest of the passwords?

First, we'll look at the case of using mostly Apple devices. Your best bet is to use the Apple provided iCloud Keychain which allows you to sign in on any web site with a username and password and have it remembered across all your Apple devices if using Safari as your web browser. Safari also can recommend very long and complicated passwords if you don't feel like thinking of one. It also allows you to store credit and debit card information, e-mail and message account info, and WiFi passwords, all encrypted both on Apple servers and while in transit to your devices.

Let's pause for a moment and digest this a bit. Access to all of your website passwords, including banking, are stored by Apple in their servers, accessible to you on your Apple devices. This is why you need a solid, impossible to guess, but easy for you to remember, password on your phone, computer, iPad, and for your Apple ID, which is your key to logging into Apple's iCloud service where these passwords are stored and retrieved.

To some, this may sound risky, but the alternative is likely worse, like using the same password for everything or writing them all down on a piece of paper which can get lost or stolen. I also don't recommend the easy option of "logging in with Facebook, Google or Linked-in" in order to log onto another site. If this password were ever hacked, you'll have a hard time knowing which other services are now also vulnerable. It is much better to have a username and password for each web site and store them in iCloud Keychain. The list of passwords can be seen on your iPhone or Mac computer should you ever need to look one of them up, like in the next example.

There is one caveat to using iCloud keychain. Currently, if you were to log into an account on your computer using Safari and then use the same app on your smartphone, you will have to put in the password at least once in the app to log you in. More and more phone apps however are using the Touch ID feature (where a fingerprint is the password) to log in, so if your app supports that, using Touch ID for apps on your phone is a great way to go and is one of many biometric security techniques likely in the future. More innovation is certain to come in this very important area.

It may be the case that you have non-Apple phones or computers and want to use a password manager that works across multiple platforms. Two popular ones are LastPass and 1Password, both of which have some cost associated with their use but work across Mac, PC, iPhone, Android, and Windows. I would encourage you to do your own evaluation of these products before choosing one. I use iCloud Keychain because I am currently using all Apple products.

Security is now and always will be a never-ending game of cat and mouse. Hackers usually target vulnerable, high value, or celebrity targets so try not to be one, and make good common-sense decisions.

Bottom Line - Basics

Set up your Internet service, using your own router and modem with both 2.4GHz and 5GHz networks, each with their own unique name, and have your computer and smartphone set up to connect to either one of the networks. Use WPA Personal security for WiFi using the same password for both networks.

Run speedtests on your computer on speedtest.net and with your smartphone using the Ookla speedtest app and know what your upload and download results are. Make sure that the upload and download measurements are at least what you are paying for from your ISP.

Using speedtest on your smartphone, evaluate any location in your home you anticipate putting a Smart Home device to ensure you have good WiFi service. If you find dead-spots, you'll have to move the router around or extend the network with another router acting as a wireless extender.

To manage and keep track of the usernames and passwords you have accumulated, use a password manager like iCloud Keychain to create unique complex passwords for each site. Do not log on with Facebook or other services as a shortcut. There are only a handful of passwords you will have to commit to memory.

If you set up a guest wireless network for friends who pop over, the password should be different than the one you use for your primary WiFi network. If you have a mixed environment of PC's or Android phones, you'll probably want to pick a third party trusted password manager with similar functionality to iCloud Keychain.

Congratulations for making it to this point! It's not so hard, is it? Laying the groundwork for the cool things to come will pay great dividends because when you start installing the things that you really care about, *they'll actually work!*

Part B - Music & Photos

If any of the following items are still a part of your home experience, then this part of the book is for you:

- Huge expensive complicated music playback systems
- Music CDs
- Cassette tapes
- 35mm negatives or slides
- Printed photos stored in shoe boxes
- Stacks of photo albums

Now that you have built the foundation for a Smart Home, you can also use it to simplify and declutter both your Music and Photo libraries.

If you just can't wait to move on to the Smart Home section, that's OK too. You can come back to this section any time.

Chapter 6 – Streaming Music

Of all things digital, music and photography have changed the most over the past twenty years. Where now you can store massive amounts of music, or stream it, on just about any device, the days of heavy duty hardware don't feel that far in the past. It feels like yesterday that I set up the ultimate music system to play my albums (also known as vinyl records or LPs), Compact Disks (CD) and cassette tapes. For that I needed a record player, a CD player, a cassette tape player, a tuner (for radio stations), and a nice big amplifier all in one stack next to the collection of albums and CDs so that I would have an amazing sound system that'd be the envy of the neighborhood. And all *that* stuff was dwarfed by the massive speaker set that somehow felt necessary to justify the amplifier stack.

If you still have any of this, then this chapter should help you free up some precious real estate in your home. (If you want to! I'm not talking down to the modern turntable set here!) Music moved from vinyl and cassette to a digital format with CDs in the 1990s but with the advent of the Internet and digital music players, the older forms of music playback have become obsolete. The next major shift happened in the early 2000s — people could buy individual songs online rather than buying complete albums. Most people are still familiar with doing something like this on iTunes and then putting the songs onto their iPod or phone for playback. But that is quickly becoming old school, too.

Music rental is replacing music ownership. Why bother buying a thousand songs for $1000 when you can rent thirty million songs for $10 per month? Music services like Pandora, Spotify, Apple Music and others have negated the need to buy music and if you are lazy like me when it comes to putting together playlists, you can let the music services do it for you.

That is a lot of change for twenty years, and many people wonder how their music setup should look to best take advantage of this transformation. The first thing to note is that virtually every song you ever had in your LP, CD, or cassette collection is now available from a music service. You can throw them all away or sell them and still have every song and album you want, on any of your devices by subscribing to something like Apple Music or Spotify. Subscription to Pandora, a service that curates your music based on your tastes, are free or without ads for about $55 per year.

Music inside the home

Remember the towering stack of equipment and speakers? Gone. Now you can enjoy music in every room, virtually an unlimited selection, and control it all simply from your smartphone or computer. The sound quality is incredible, it's so easy to operate that every member of your family will use it all the time without any instruction.

There is more than one way to do this but I will share my setup with you that I have had for well over seven years and is probably the best money I have spent on any kind of electronics. There is a very ordinary looking and nondescript music system that you will see in a bunch of stores called Sonos, a company based out of Southern California. When I saw the system in the store, it didn't jump out at me as being all that impressive but a smart friend of mine had it and when I was describing my music challenges, he said, "Trust me. Just get it. It is the best thing ever." So, I did, and he was right. I am using Sonos as an example here but there are other wireless sound systems from the likes of Bose and Sony with similar capabilities.

First, let's assume you have nothing at all in the house for music (no speakers, no wiring, no tuner, etc.) There are a series of "all in 1" speakers that you just plug into an electrical outlet. They all connect over the WiFi network that you've already set up in your home, and they're controlled with the Sonos app that you download on your phone, tablet, or computer. With Sonos and other similar systems, you get virtually every radio station on earth from a service called TuneIn. Just select your station and it plays. You also have the option of subscribing to music services like Pandora, Satellite Radio, Spotify, Apple Music, and many others. It is so intuitive and simple that there's no point in even describing how to do it since you will figure it out on your own in sixty seconds. The various speaker systems come in three sizes (small, medium, large) which roughly correspond to how much you want pay and the size of the rooms you want to put the speaker(s) in. It's dead simple to pair two or more of these to create stereo or even surround sound should you wish. You can play something different in each room you set up, or you can group places in your house together to play music perfectly in synch across multiple rooms. Walk out of the kitchen singing and enter the living room without missing a beat.

If you already have a set of speakers that you want to use, Sonos also offers an amplifier unit that physically wires to those speakers and transforms them into a room zone. I wired a couple of all-weather outdoor speakers in the back yard and use the Sonos Amplifier to drive those as my outdoor zone. They also have sound bars for wall mount TVs and a base stand for TVs on a stand, and subwoofers if you really want your house to shake. Software updates are as simple and elegant as I have seen in the industry. The price may *seem* expensive but, the equipment lasts forever and there is a solid resale market should you choose to upgrade. There are other top name brands that now have similar systems, so of course research and choose what is best for you.

Most importantly, you can do all this yourself and it's all wireless so you don't need to pay anyone to rummage in the attic with a spool of speaker wire.

Music on the go

Again, there are a couple of different ways to listen to music when you're not in the home, using the same music services that you have running through a Sonos or equivalent system. The easiest way to explain how to do this is by example. In my case, I have an old library of songs that I had purchased either on CD or through iTunes that sits on my Mac at home and is accessible through the iTunes application on my computer. Since I always synch my iPhone with my Mac, the songs that are in my iTunes library on my computer are also available on my iPhone. So, by pressing the Music button on my phone, I can listen to all the music that I own through earbuds or some other device that it's plugged into. For example, our car has a USB jack and by plugging in my iPhone in the car, it not only charges the phone but also acts as the playback for any music played from the phone. But you don't have to physically plug in your phone if your car supports Bluetooth. If so, wirelessly pair your phone with the Bluetooth in your car and it has the same music streaming capability as plugging your phone into the USB port.

Many newer cars support Apple CarPlay or Android Auto that fully integrates smartphone functions with the car's in dash display. This makes music playback simpler but also many other functions that you shouldn't be doing on your phone while driving anyway. If your car supports this, you should use it. If you are shopping for a new car, look carefully at the fine print and consider adding this feature to your next set of wheels.

The second example are the music streaming services that you subscribe to using your Sonos system at home like Pandora, Apple Music, Spotify, and SiriusXM. By simply downloading those respective apps onto your iPhone, and logging into the same accounts as you use on Sonos, you have access to all the same music on your phone as you travel. Some services like Spotify and Apple Music also allow you to listen in "offline" mode whereby you can download songs of your choice to your iPhone and listen to them locally when you have no Internet connection, such as when you're on an airplane and you don't want to pay for WiFi. And, when you are in the car, playing music from any of the streaming services you have access to on your phone works the same way either through a physical USB connection or Bluetooth.

Your smartphone is the hub of your music experience when you are outside the home. It contains the songs you own plus access to all the libraries from all of the streaming services you subscribe to, and you can play them on anything your smartphone can connect to. What's the catch? As you know by now, when data goes into or out of your smartphone, it may count against your cellular monthly data limits. Sometimes, music streaming will not count against your data plan depending on your carrier and there are trends towards higher capacity data plans where it becomes almost impossible to hit your data limits or you may even have an unlimited data plan. So, make sure you know what kind of data plan you have and what the rules are for streaming music. These plans tend to change like the seasons, so keep checking back to make sure your plan meets your needs. As an example, I have a data plan that allows me 10GB per month per phone. Even in months when I have been traveling and not using WiFi, I've barely used 2GB, but everyone will be different. Be aware that streaming video over a cellular phone can get eat up a lot of data, so keep tabs on it through your service provider's website. Remember that when you use your smartphone on your WiFi, no data charges will apply against your cellular data plan.

Bottom Line - Music

What to do

For your in-home music, if you want it, you won't have to deal with any more LPs, CDs, cassettes, or towers of expensive gear. Only a few Sonos (or equivalent) room speakers controlled by an app on your phone, and you can play just about any song ever recorded as well as listen to any radio station in the world. All this across your WiFi network and Internet connection that you have already installed for your Smart Home. And yes, if you do have songs still on your iPhone or Android, you can play them, too.

The music hub for outside the home is your smartphone. All of the music services that you can stream through your in-home system are available on your phone, so whether you play music off the Internet or from your own playlists, it's all there. Your output device can be ear pods, connecting through your Car's wireless Bluetooth (or wired USB) or even at someone else's home, through their wireless system.

Budget

The lower end smart speaker models start at about $200 with the higher end in the $400 to $700 range. The amount you spend is really dictated by the number of places in and around the home that you want hear your music in.

$400-700 seemed like a lot of money to spend on a sound system until I stumbled on a receipt from 1997 for a tuner/amplifier that I bought for $1200 to pair with an equally expensive set of speakers.

As with most aspects of your Smart Home project, it makes sense to start small, get comfortable, and then expand when the desire and budget permits.

Chapter 7 – Enjoying your Photos

Once upon a time, to get your picture taken, you had to go to a studio and sit still in some good lighting for a couple of minutes as a professional photographer took your likeness. After bathing the negative in a series of chemical baths, the image was finished. At the very beginning, the result was just a single positive, printed on glass or tin. Now your phone can take fifty pictures in one second of your kid making a 3-pointer. And five seconds later, you can send any number of them anywhere in the world.

Now, as a species of avid digital photographers, we have new challenges. We don't develop our photos and put them in albums very much anymore, which is a pity, because we probably took more pleasure in our photographs when we didn't take fifty a day. (Or in the case of the SnapChat/selfie-obsessed younger generation, fifty an hour.)

It may not be uncommon to have almost 20,000 digital photos that are organized and another 20,000 that are in a digital "pile" still waiting for some structure so you can actually *look* at them... An unorganized set of digital photos is pretty much useless because if nobody is enjoying them, they might as well not have been taken in the first place. The goal of this chapter, then, is to find easy and creative ways to bring new life to your photo collection and to enjoy them in ways that made all those hours of picture-taking worthwhile.

People typically fall into two eras when it comes to taking pictures. If you started taking photos only in the past few years, it's likely that all of your pictures are digital. (I know there are still legions of camera fans and pros who still use film, but even you folks can make and keep digital back-ups of your photographs.)

When you take a photo with your smartphone, it automatically attaches its location, date and time taken, along with other so-called metadata information. Photographs taken with a smartphone are automatically organized. If you were taking photographs any time before 2002, though, you probably have shoeboxes of printed pictures, negatives, and slides which may be nice and organized but more likely in a state of total chaos. If you want to include those photos in your new digitally organized world, it's possible, but it's certainly more work and expense.

Let's start with the first kind of photographer, the one who can talk to his mother on his camera, and I'll use an iPhone as an example.

Keeping Photos in Sync

By far, the easiest way to manage your photos is to let your phone and computer do all the work. If you let the Photos app built into your iPhone organize your pictures, you should have them in neat order, synchronized across all your devices (smartphone, tablet, computer). The Photos app uses the data attached to each picture and organizes it into something called "moments". Experiment with this and you will see how powerful it is to be able to find photos, tag them with people's faces, automatically have them plotted on a map of where they were taken, etc. Your phone, however, has a limited amount of memory and at some point, you'll exhaust it and you won't be able to take any more photos. Fortunately, there is an easy solution for this, too, and it's the reason you enabled iCloud earlier when you set up your phone and computer.

On your iPhone settings under iCloud and Photos, make sure you have "My Photo Stream" and "iCloud Photo Sharing" turned on. There is another setting for "iCloud Photo Library" that I would leave off until you get a good handle on the overall size of your photo library. If you have a large collection of photos, you may use up the free 5GB of storage Apple gives you on the iCloud. (Not to mention that uploading a 20,000 picture library on a 5Mbps Internet uplink would take some twenty-nine hours while using your entire Internet connection). When you turn on those two settings, every picture you take on your iPhone is automatically uploaded (when connected to WiFi) to your very own storage space in Apple's iCloud. When you open the included Photos app on your Apple computer, these photos automatically show up in your photos app so that everything taken on your phone is also available on the computer. No removing memory cards, e-mailing pictures to yourself, or any other tricks. Note that this linkage of photos and the storage space in Apple's iCloud is directly connected to your Apple ID, so make sure that every device you want to auto-feed photos into is logged into the same Apple ID. Of course, since you are regularly backing up your computer using Time Machine, you have a double backup copy of the photos taken on your phone.

Now, what happens when your phone is full of photos? Since all of these photos are on your computer (please check first), you can delete photos on your phone to make more memory available. I encourage you to experiment with the Photos app on the computer. It's very easy to create albums, movies, and picture books as gifts, as well as to tag photos with people's names and faces, making it easy to create customized collections.

Photos from the Shoebox

This is a hard-core undertaking. But if you have years of photographs and/or slides, this will be the last time you'll ever have to sort them. The onerous part of the job is finding all your old photos, negatives, and slides, and converting them to a digital format that you can import into Photos on your Mac. This methodology also applies if you are using another type of photo organization application on the Mac or PC.

There are multiple ways of getting these older photos into a digital format. If you just have a few you want to do, any of the following ways will work fine although they are all fairly labor intensive.

If you have printed photos, and you can take a picture of the photo with your phone, this is probably the easiest and fastest way. Pay careful attention try to avoid glare from overhead lighting or the sun, and don't cast your own shadow on the photo either. Once you have mastered the technique for getting these shots straight on and you like the look, they essentially become photos taken from your phone and will automatically show up in Photos on the Mac. Note that these will likely require some editing and the date and location will be tagged incorrectly, so you'll want to fix that as well, which I'll cover in a bit.

Again, for printed photos, if you have a scanner and an easy way to get the scanned photos into your computer from the scanner, this is another option. These scanned photos will likely end up in a digital pile somewhere in a folder on your computer so there is an extra step (an easy one) to import the photos into the Photos Application which will then also require the same editing that the first conversion method does.

If you have 35mm negatives, you can purchase a machine to scan these and put them in digital format but a much better choice is to go to a Photo service that will do this for you. If you used Advanced Photo System (APS) film, you have little choice but to use a service since that film type is long obsolete and buying a conversion device is cost prohibitive.

However you choose to convert from physical format to digital, the two pieces of information that you'll want to carry across are the date the photo was taken and the location. I mentioned earlier about needing to edit the photos when they are brought into the Photos Application. Here are the considerations around editing that may influence how you go about getting them converted.

If you took pictures of pictures or scanned them, you will likely have to edit every picture (one by one) in two ways, all in the Photos app on the Mac. The picture will likely need the edges cropped and perhaps a slight rotation to align it properly. This is very easily done in the app along with doing touchups to get rid of artifacts if you so choose. While this is easy and even fun, it is VERY time consuming so if you have hundreds or thousands of photos to do, you will probably want to skip this step by choosing to use a photo conversion service that will align and crop for you.

You might remember reading about metadata information contained with each digital photo, in particular the date and location that the photo was taken. Whether self-converted or done by a service, both of these are initially going to be wrong. If using a service, ask them what date they will be tagged with, or you may be able to specify a date so that when imported, they will be easy to find and change once in Photos. With the service I used, I was able to ask them to do the following:

- Put the digital scans of each set of negatives in their own folder with a name that corresponded to what I wrote on the sheet of negatives. If I knew the approximate date or year the photos were taken, I wrote that on the envelope. This way, each set of negatives was grouped together and it made it easier to change the date and location once in Photos on the Mac.
- For negatives that were scattered or not part of a known set, I had them labelled as "untagged" but still grouped in the piles that I found them in. The hope was that they were related to each other and would be easier to sort later.
- For APS photos, the date of processing is recorded in the cartridge, so I had them use that to date the digital versions.
- I chose a resolution that would yield similar results as if I took the photo with my iPhone today. Those numbers are represented differently by the various photo services but you want them in the range of

3000 dpi (dots per inch) or 10MP (megapixels). Use the JPEG format as that's the format your phone uses. Sometimes TIFF formats are offered but unless you know why you would want that, you probably don't.

If you send in negatives, there are going to be some duds that you wish you hadn't paid them to scan. Many services offer you the option of previewing the scanned photos online before committing to the ones that you will actually get and allow you to delete and not pay for a bunch (some have limits in the 20% range - read the fine print). This is a nice option if you are not sure of the content of your negatives. When it is all said and done, you will end up with a disk drive or some kind of set of files that should be organized by folders, possibly with dates the pictures were taken on the folders. Now is the job of getting these photos into your Photos application and organized with dates and location tags.

There are many ways to do this, but I would recommend importing one folder at a time and once that folder is imported all the photos from that folder show up on the screen and are ready for editing for date and location. You can edit for exact date and time to the second, but it is probably more important just to have them in the correct order so approximate dates to the month are probably good enough. It's possible to select multiple photos at once to change the date and location. Just use the "Image" pulldown and choose "Adjust date and time". Make sure you use the latest version of Photos before changing the date because it was quite awkward in the first version of the product and much easier now. The location is changed by first choosing "Info" under the "Windows" pulldown and then clicking on the "add a location" field. You can type addresses or places just like you were using Google Maps or similar. Again, if multiple photos were taken at the same place, you can select them all and set their location all at once.

So, why bother with all of this manual work? Well, if you are going to the trouble and expense of converting all these photos, you might as well take the extra time to organize them by date and location because Photos will use that information to automatically organize them. The way Photos structures your library makes it very easy to put together albums and slideshows. You'll thank yourself later for doing it!

What does it cost to get your photos converted? First, I would encourage you to explore different services but in general, pricing is in the 20¢ to 40¢ range per image that you want to keep. Like I said earlier, this is a project in and of itself, but once done, you have these in digital format forever.

<u>Enjoying your Photos</u>

The whole purpose of taking photos is to enjoy them at a later date, so now that they're organized, our computers will do most of the work to present them to us in a simple and usable fashion. I am not going to cover how to show people pictures on your phone because you already know how to do that, nor how to post them on your favorite social media accounts for sharing. What we will cover are a couple of new and easy ways to display and share that may not be so obvious.

Making Movies from Photos

My wife and I went on a long cycling trip a few years back and at the end of each week, one of the people on the trip sent out a "picture movie" of the week complete with a nice music track that lasted 4-5 minutes. We were all so impressed with his technical prowess that he became somewhat of a movie-making tech genius. I asked him about this one evening and he laughed and said that it only took him a few minutes using Photos on his Mac to put the whole thing together.

Here is how you can do this too. When you open Photos, you will see all your pictures organized by date, along with any shared libraries and albums that you may have created. To create a movie, simply select "Create Slideshow" under the File menu and then select a bunch of pictures that you want to be part of the slideshow. That's it!! Now preview it and see what it looks like. Change any pictures, the order of pictures, music, timing etc. by clicking on the various icons to the right of the screen. This slideshow movie is saved in your Photos app on the left side under the heading of "Projects" so you can always come back and edit it later and create a new version. When you are satisfied with it, click on the Export button on the top right to save it as a movie that you can then share, post on YouTube, or just put on your phone for personal enjoyment.

If you have already created albums inside your photo library, it is also pretty easy to create a movie from an album. Just click on the album, select the pictures you want and then use "create slideshow" and those pictures will be used to start off the video. It literally takes seconds to do this, so it's ok to make mistakes as they are easily fixed.

Playing Photos on your TV

I'd been wanting for years to put a nice flat screen TV right above the fireplace in the living room but it didn't pass muster with my wife until one day she had the idea to use it as a giant picture frame to view photos from our photo library.

A long time ago, we had a small digital picture frame that used a SD memory card to load photos for viewing. I dutifully added a bunch of pictures to the card after one of our trips, stuck it in the picture frame and it played over and over again. Once bored with that picture loop, I put it on my list to load some new photos on the card, but for some reason I never did. There had to be something less cumbersome than transferring photos to a picture frame on an SD card. It took a few more years, but now there is a very easy way to do it, and it involves using something that we'll want later for our Smart Home project (if we choose to use Apple's HomeKit): A 4th generation Apple TV or Apple TV 4K if you have a 4K TV. You may be used to using Apple TV for renting movies, watching Netflix, YouTube, or any number of other video, music, sports, and news services that are available, but there is a Photos app on Apple TV as well.

In the Photos app on either your iPhone or Mac computer, you'll see a folder called "Shared". Anything in this folder will be stored in Apple's iCloud, and can be viewed on any Apple device logged into the same Apple ID, or by any user you have shared the pictures with. The easiest way to do this is to create a new shared album on your phone or computer and add at least one other user to it (I add my wife) and then you will both see that shared album on your devices. You can both add pictures to the albums, and you can add other users, like far flung family members, if you want to share and build your photo albums with them as well.

Now that you have these shared albums created (kids, Europe trip, Christmas Photos, Pet photos, etc.), you want to be able to view them on your TV. With your Apple TV logged into the Apple ID that you used to create the shared albums, you can now see all of them by selecting the Photos app on Apple TV and looking for the albums under "My Albums". Select one and run slideshow and you now have your pictures playing on your TV. You can play with the settings to adjust the timing and transitions to your liking. Also, if someone else initially created the shared album but they added you, you will find those pictures in albums under the "Shared Albums" heading in the Photos app on Apple TV. And, all these shared albums will also appear on all your Apple devices allowing you to view or add to the libraries as you see fit.

So, if Grandma lives far away and you want to surprise her with all the latest grandkid's photos and perhaps she is not so tech savvy, a simple Apple TV, a few clicks and she can view all the latest photos just by adding her as another subscriber to your shared albums. You add the pictures, and she turns on the TV to view them!

Feel free to experiment with the slideshow settings on AppleTV. The rectangular shape of pictures is a different size than the flat screen TV so they will not fit exactly. If you choose Classic mode, none of the picture will get cut off, but you won't fill the screen widthwise. If you choose the Ken Burns effect, your pictures will fill the whole screen and transition with the Burns' scroll-and-zoom effect. There is always a setting that will work for the type of pictures you have so don't be afraid to experiment.

Bottom Line - Enjoying your Photos

What to Do

Use a program like Photos on your Mac to organize and synchronize all the photos you've taken with your smartphones and tablets. Make sure all the Apple devices that you use to view the photos are signed on to the same Apple ID. For older photos, negatives, and slides, choose a photo conversion service that will convert them all to digital, and then import the files into Photos to add you your library. You will likely need to edit the date and location of the photos imported to organize them properly. If you only have a small number to convert, you can do this yourself by taking a picture of the picture or using a scanner.

Once you have a working library, use the Photos app on your computer to create simple photo movies to share with others. Also, create shared albums with others and use Apple TV or Apple TV 4K (if you have a 4K TV) to display your photos on the big screen.

Budget

The Photos app on the Mac is free as is the first 5GB of storage in iCloud for photos. Photo conversion will cost about 20¢ to 40¢ per photo or negative. A fourth generation (or later) Apple TV is in the $150 range and it will be the same product used later in the Smart Home part of the book for using the Apple

HomeKit app to control and schedule many of your smart devices.

Result

Most people are pretty impressed to see photos playing on the TV and since most of this was done with things already part of the Smart Home project, it was an easy and fun thing to do involving all the family members.

Part C - Smart Home Solutions

This part of the book is broken into ten Chapters, each detailing how to add another piece of Smart Home technology to your house. The end of each chapter provides a "Bottom Line" or summary, so if you are anxious to get going quickly, jump to the end of the chapter to get started. An important part of building a Smart Home with many different product types is figuring out an elegant way to use it on a day-to-day basis with all of the app choices available. Each chapter introduces some of these choices and makes recommendations of how to keep things simple. Chapter 18 dives more into the app choices and strategies and Chapter 19 gives some tips on what to do if you move out of or into a Smart Home.

Speaking of moving, it might be the last thing on your mind, but when it does happen, there's an easy way to keep the Smart Home part of the move low stress. See the sidebar on this page for a quick to-do before you tackle the next set of chapters.

Have fun with this. I am certain that you will impress yourself with what you create.

> **Do This Now**
>
> Create a new e-mail address that you will only use for the Smart Home project. Use it as the e-mail account on all Smart Home Products. When you move, you will give it away to the new buyer and save hours of time not having to un-install and re-install your Smart Home products.

Chapter 8 – Lighting

Lighting used to be simple. There was a bulb and there was a switch and there were two settings: on and off. Occasionally, if things got fancy, a lamp might have a bulb with three different levels of brightness or the chandelier above the dining room table would have a dimmer switch installed so you could set the mood. Maybe you had one of those vacation timers (that box with the big dial you'd plug into the wall to operate your lights when you went away). Outside landscape lighting would run off a low voltage lighting system with an automatic timer that you'd go out and adjust for the changing sunset times throughout the season. Light bulbs were easy to buy with 90% of them being the frosted white incandescent type at either 40, 60 or 100 watts.

But then things started changing. Electricity rates started to take a bigger chunk out of the pocketbook and people began to compare the costs of running these relatively high wattage incandescent bulbs with some of the newer options, initially Compact Fluorescent Lights (CFL) and later Light Emitting Diode (LED) bulbs. At the same time, with new

Smart Home technology, the possibility of automating many or all of the switches and plugs is another enticing option.

It can be a daunting task to figure out a cost effective, simple to use, and practical solution for your lighting needs. It begins the moment you start shopping for light bulbs. A task that was once so simple — you could buy lightbulbs at the grocery store! — these days can be a genuine challenge when you're confronted with the choices you have.

This chapter will cut through the guesswork when it comes to putting together an integrated solution for lighting that is simple to buy, easy to set up yourself, and sets the stage for other aspects of your Smart Home design in subsequent chapters.

Lighting Strategy

Starting with inside lighting, there are a few things to consider from a design perspective. As described near the beginning of the book, we want anything automated to be controlled both from the wall switch and from a smartphone. The smartphone control allows for simple programming of moods, light levels, and timing and it means that if anyone walks into a room and doesn't have a clue that they're in a Smart Home, they'll still be able to control the lights from the wall switches with no special instruction. With that in mind, we need to cover a few things about the light bulbs themselves.

Consider that any or all of your bulbs can be either dimmable or not. We'll assume for all practical purposes that we'll be using LED bulbs and that dimmable bulbs are more expensive than non-dimmable ones, but not by much. If you're going the budget route, plan to use all non-dimmable bulbs except for the couple of spots in the house where they'd really make a difference, like the dining room. I chose to get all dimmable bulbs to simplify sparing and also because the slight cost increase still amounts to very little. If there are situations where you want colored lighting, it's possible, but if you want them as part of your Smart Home system, they're expensive: around $50 each. The implications of these so called smart bulbs are covered in a few pages.

Now comes a major decision. Which lights in your home do you want to be part of your Smart Home system? This will determine how many Smart Home switches you need. As of this writing, normal light switches cost about $5 while a Smart Home switch is about $50. Automating your entire home can be an expensive proposition, but you can start small and grow as the budget permits.

Buying an LED Light Bulb

Whoever would have imagined that this was a subject worth writing about? But it is, because with LED bulbs, there are many more choices than we've ever had in the past.

We're used to buying regular incandescent light bulbs that offer us two choices: wattage (brightness) — and bulb shape.

Newer LED bulbs add a few more things including some differences in terminology:

- **LED brightness** is measured in **lumens**, although LED bulbs are still sold by "wattage equivalent" for comparison's sake. A "60W" LED bulb should give you the same brightness as a 60W incandescent bulb.
- The **color temperature** of the bulb (e.g. soft white, daylight, measured in Kelvins)
- **Dimmable** or non-dimmable
- **Switch compatibility** for dimming (not all dimmable LEDs work with all dimmers)
- **Smart bulbs** or not

Brightness

When replacing incandescent bulbs with LEDs, match the wattage if you want to keep lighting levels where you're used to them being, but note that there are some minor differences (like 800 or 815 lumens) when you look at different LED brands. If you want uniformity of lighting, stick with one brand.

One thing to note here is that the higher wattage equivalent LED bulbs are quite a bit more expensive than lower wattage ones. For example, my outdoor lights had 100W bulbs in them but because 100W LED bulbs were so much more expensive than their 60W versions, I went with 60W LED for the replacement and really couldn't tell much difference overall.

Light color temperature

"Temperature" is a relatively new attribute that became popular with LED bulbs. Simply put, the temperature, measured in Kelvins (e.g. 2700K, 5000K) determines the color of the light. Incandescent bulbs labeled as soft white (which is most of them) are 2700K and if you pick an LED bulb rated at 2700K, it will look the same as the incandescent bulbs you are used to. I would recommend that if you are buying replacement bulbs, get the 2700K variety and then even if you mix and match new LED with old incandescent or compact fluorescent light (CFL) bulbs, you won't notice the difference in color. The higher color temperature bulbs like 5000K may be appropriate for rooms where you want to simulate daylight. Please experiment but keep your receipts just in case.

Dimmable or non-dimmable

Every LED should be marked to tell you whether it is dimmable or not. Non-dimmable bulbs are less expensive, but dimmable ones are reasonably priced in the $4 or less range. I suspect that, over time, the price difference between dimmable and non-dimmable will converge even more, rendering non-dimmable LEDs obsolete. In my case, I chose to use all dimmable bulbs because I would never remember where each type was installed and it requires fewer bulb types to store as replacements. Also, when it comes to installing the smart switches to control the bulbs, the price of the smart dimmer switches is almost the same, if not less than non-dimmable smart switches. In a modest sized home, I would have all of the switches as smart dimmable switches so having all the bulbs as dimmable just simplifies everything.

Switch Compatibility for Dimming

When dimmable LED bulbs first came out, certain combinations of bulbs and dimmer switches did not work well together. There were lots of instances of light flickering and loud buzzing sounds when the lights were dimmed. There are plenty of combinations that will work just fine and often the bulb and dimmer manufacturers will provide lists of compatible products. In my case, I chose Caséta dimmers from Lutron (more detail in the next section) and use both Cree and Ecosmart LED bulbs available from Home Depot, Satco (most lighting stores and online) and Utilitech LED bulbs and fixtures from Lowes with no issues. Generally speaking, the generic-sized bulbs are more compatible with dimmers and I only had problems with fancy chandelier LED bulbs, some of which would not work with my chosen dimmer. Sometimes at full strength on the dimmer, LED lights of some manufacturers make a loud buzz — this is a brand problem; try another.

In general, if you have an issue with LED bulbs and dimmers, it's usually the fault of the bulb. You can verify this by testing the socket with a regular incandescent bulb and seeing if it works. The bottom line is, buy LED bulbs at a store that takes returns and if they don't work, take them back and try another brand. Once you find a brand or two that works well with your dimmers, stick to it.

Smart Bulbs (or not)

What exactly is a smart bulb? Some light bulbs (Philips Hue is a good example) have wireless technology built in and they can connect directly to a network or through a bridge to be controlled individually. The power to the light needs to be on in order for the bulb to be controlled. Because each bulb is individually controlled, you can set the color of the light one bulb at a time. (Red, green, etc.) The price of these bulbs is about 5-10x the price of regular dimmable LED bulbs, so in my opinion this makes them more of a novelty item and impractical for use through your entire house.

There may be a room or perhaps an outdoor light that you want to use a colored light in. Because its switch has to be on for these bulbs to work, you may have to manually check the on/off status of your switches if the bulbs disappear from your app. Also, if you have a switch that controls a number of bulbs, you would need to replace them all with smart bulbs in order to use them. This gets pretty expensive for even a moderate sized home so dimmer switches are a much more cost-effective strategy.

Dimmers and Timers

Before changing to a Smart Home, our home lighting inadvertently evolved into a fairly complicated setup. I installed four light timers (about $20 each) in place of wall switches in order to turn lights on and off at certain programmed times. Of course, I always forgot how to program these when the time changed or when the battery needed replacing. We had several lamp timers (forgot how to program those too) that I would plug into outlets and use for lamps and Christmas tree lights. I also had a couple of exterior plug-in switches with small remote controls that were used for outdoor lighting. Finally, we had two hanging chandelier lights with a couple of dimmer switches. What a mess! If this all sounds like a familiar starting point, you are not alone.

Our goal is to integrate all this into one system that would allow us to turn lights on and off, or dim them with a wall switch or a smartphone but *also* to be able to program a schedule centrally from any smart device using an elegant and simple interface. I also wanted to be able to do this while in my home or away. I also hoped to get maximum integration between the lighting system and other systems, like heating, fire detection, blinds, garage door, cameras, and so on. You'll see later that while it's an admirable goal, it's not simple to achieve fully. I'll walk you through the complexities of that installation, as well as the final result, which while not perfect, ended up being totally serviceable.

There are two kinds of companies that have products for lighting automation. First are the companies that have been making lighting products for years, like Lutron, Leviton, and a few others. The others are technology companies that started in Smart Home design like WeMo (Belkin), iDevices, Insteon and others.

In order to be connected and controllable by a smartphone, these devices (switches, dimmers, etc.) need to be able to communicate to the Internet in some way. Many of these small Internet appliances don't talk the same language as your smartphone and so they need to be "bridged" into your home network with a special purpose network appliance called, oddly enough, a bridge! Some of these special languages or protocols you will see on labels are names like ZigBee, Z-wave, ClearConnect, and others. Some devices also use WiFi and do not need any kind of bridge. In the end, it really doesn't matter too much as long as it works reliably and that you don't end up with a huge stack of bridges to put somewhere near your router.

As mentioned before, each vendor is going to have its own app and while many are vying to be the "king of the castle" app that you will use every day, many apps allow other devices to integrate into it as well as allowing its devices to integrate into other apps. One of the candidate apps to be "king of the castle" if you are an iPhone user is the Home app that works on every iPhone running version 10.1 or later (October 2016). Any product that works with the Apple Home app is called "HomeKit compatible" and since we are iPhone users, I want to select quality products that are HomeKit compatible to evaluate whether the Apple app is a good one to use at the top of the app hierarchy. Before solving that, we'll take a quick diversion into some lighting terminology so the rest of this chapter makes sense.

Light Switch Terminology

If you've never opened up a light switch and looked at the wiring, this section will be new to you. If you have, then consider it a refresher. There are a few different types of light switches so it is important to know what you have before you replace them with smart switches.

Single Pole Switches

This is the simplest setup. A single switch controls a light or a set of lights. There is a total of three physical wires going to this switch (ground, plus two others). The majority of the light switches in a house will be of this type.

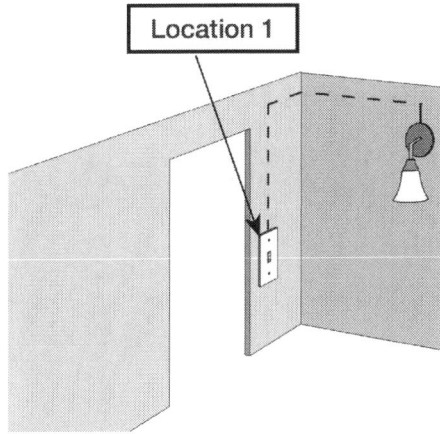

Location 1

Three-way Switch

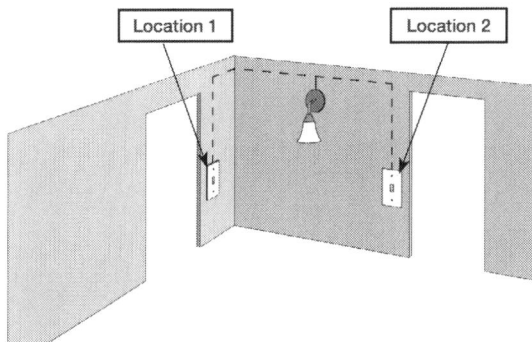

Location 1   Location 2

This setup allows a set of lights to be controlled by either of two different switches. In this switch, there are a total of four wires (ground plus three others) going to each of the two switches. The switches look the same on the outside but are physically different inside in order to accommodate the extra wires needed to do three-way switching.

Multi-location switch

If there are three or more switches controlling the same set of lights, you'll see a minimum of five wires (one ground and four others). Again, this

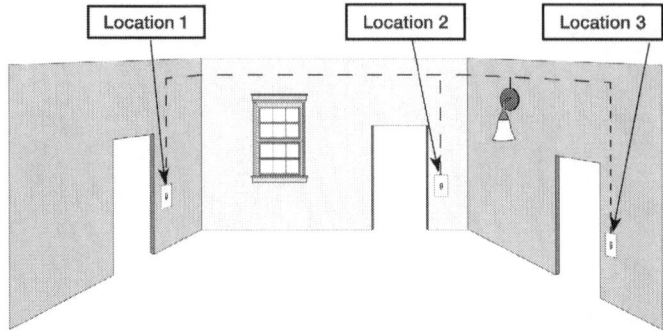

is yet a different switch type than the previous two.

These are all things that electricians need to think about when devising a wiring plan for your home. They have to select the correct switches, install a wire with the right number of conductors, and hook it all up correctly. Luckily — presuming you're not in the process of rewiring your home — this part of the process is complete and all you have to do is identify which type of switch you have at each location so that you know what to replace it with. Fortunately, you don't have to open them up to do this - just figure out how many different switches can turn each set of lights on and off.

When replacing the old switches with some new programmable smart dimmers, you can use the same dimmer in all three cases and just follow along the instructions from the manufacturer on how to deal with the three-way and multi-location scenarios. This one of the reasons that I chose the Lutron Caséta wireless products for the lighting part of my Smart Home. In addition to elegantly handling all of these scenarios, they are Apple HomeKit compatible, have extensive testing with LED bulb manufacturers, and have been in the lighting business for a long time. They also have a very clever solution for three-way and multi-location switching that uses a wireless remote control, called a Pico Remote, that also mounts nicely into the second or third switches.

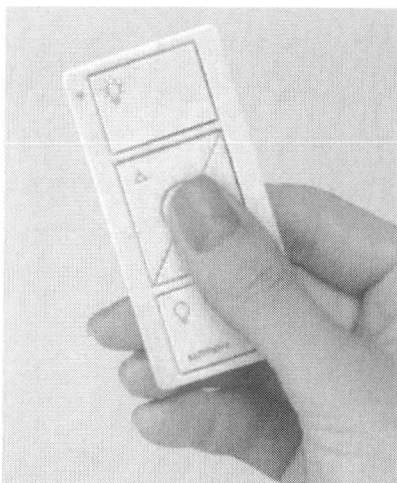

One other decision is how to handle indoor lamps, Christmas lights etc. that are plugged into an interior outlet. The choice is to replace the electrical outlet with a smart outlet, or use a lamp adapter that plugs into a regular outlet that can then be controlled in a similar manner as the smart dimmer switches described earlier. I chose to use the lamp adapter also from the Lutron Caséta line of products as it integrates seamlessly, but more importantly, when lamps get moved around the house, I don't have to rewire plugs. It just takes one minute to rename the lamp adapter and anyone can move them around. Also, if for whatever reason the lamp plugs into a Ground Fault Circuit Interrupter (GFCI) outlet in a bathroom, kitchen, laundry room, or other indoor room, will work just fine.

GFCI outlets are the ones that have the red and black test and reset buttons on the front of them. These are installed in areas near where you can touch water and in all outdoor sockets. They are there for safety reasons so you don't get electrocuted if you dry your hair over a full sink of water and drop the running dryer into the water. (Don't do this! Just take my word for it.)

Outdoor devices

If your house is safely wired, all your outdoor outlets will be of the GFCI type so if you want to control landscape lighting, outdoor Christmas lights, or other outdoor electrical plugs, the best bet is to find and use an exterior device similar to the indoor lamp dimmer that can plug into an existing outlet and then be controlled for on/off. In my case, I needed three of these for landscape lighting, Christmas lights, and some other lights we have in the backyard hanging in a Pergola.

Ideally, I would have liked to get the Lutron Caséta models but they don't make them, so as I pointed out in the beginning of this book, the more devices you connect, the more vendors become part of the mix and then integrating the products becomes a challenging part of the project. Because I anticipate using Apple's Home app, I looked for something that was HomeKit compatible, operating under the theory that using the Home app would negate the multivendor concern. I found a HomeKit enabled outdoor switch from iDevices on sale and ordered three of them. From an integration perspective, it worked out the way I had hoped. I'll explain those details after a quick safety reminder.

Electrical wiring and safety

You may have guessed by now that if you are replacing wired light switches with dimmers (the Lutron Caséta dimmer in my case), it requires exposing, disconnecting and reconnecting electric wires (of the 120-Volt variety). So, it is extremely important that you read and follow the manufacturer's directions so that you can perform this safely. In order to prepare you, a quick simplified primer on electricity is in order.

> Nobody likes to read safety information, but I hope you take a minute to read the Electricity 101 section. It might be shocking if you don't.

Electricity 101

If you take the face plate off a light switch or plug receptacle and look at the wires, you will see a black, a white, and a bare copper wire (sometimes green). In more complicated situations like three-way or multi-way switches, there will also be a red and/or blue wire.

At least one of these wires is going to be "hot", which means that if you touch it, you'll get shocked. The only thing a hot wire wants to do is to find a path to ground, so if any conductor gives it a pathway, the electrical current will take it. If you're that conductor, it will flow through you. This is *not* something you want to experience. To prevent that, here are some basic safety steps that you should always take when working with electrical wiring.

- Always turn off the power at the breaker panel if you are going to open up a switch or plug and expose the wires. This will take the hotness out of all the wires in that circuit.
- Buy a voltage detector from the store that you can use to double check if there any hot wires. Always test it first on a plug that you know is hot so that you know the detector is working. If you know how to use a digital voltmeter, you can use this for testing as well.
- While it is most often the black wire that is hot, assume all are hot since wires often get painted or sprayed and may all look white.
- If you open up a receptacle with multiple switches inside, do not assume that all of the other switches are cold even if you turned the breaker off for the one you are working on. Turn all the switches on

inside the box and turn all of the breakers off for all of the lights. Test them all with your voltage tester.

- Wear insulated shoes (not bare feet) and if you are on a ladder, try to avoid using a metal ladder. This is an extra safety measure in the event you didn't read the last page and there are hot wires in the box you are working on.
- Wearing insulating gloves is also not a bad idea if you can still manipulate tools and wires. Doing this has saved me a few times from getting shocked.

While all this might scare you, it is really not all that difficult to do the wiring yourself. Once again, read the manufacturer directions carefully. Lutron's directions are excellent and there are some advanced scenarios on their web site for more complicated situations like three-way and multi-way switches.

If at all in doubt while working with electrical wires, turn off the main breaker in your house to ensure no power is flowing to any outlets while you're working. Also, any electrician will be able to do this work if you decide you want nothing to do with wires.

Putting it all together

After the physical installation of the lamp dimmers and in-wall dimmers, you will have followed all the instructions for a standalone installation. This means that you can use the lights from the switch but not from the phone yet. Again, the instructions are simple and self-explanatory with the Lutron devices but I would add one tip that could save you some time. When you initially test each dimmer, start with regular incandescent bulbs just to make sure the dimmer works properly. The reason is that if you have CFLs, chances are that they are not dimmable and it might look like the switch isn't working when it probably is. Also, although you will ultimately find dimmable LED's that are compatible with your dimmer, some are not and you could be fooled into thinking the switch isn't working. If you don't have any incandescent bulbs lying around, it's OK to use LED bulbs to test but if you have problems, it can be tough to figure out what went wrong.

After you've ensured the dimmer is working, install the final bulb type that you desire and test the dimmer again, running it from fully off to fully on and then dimming it in increments to off. If you are using LED bulbs, listen for an annoying buzzing sound, and if you hear one and it bothers you, return the bulbs and try a different brand. (Don't worry, you will find one) When you are dimming the bulb and it is on very low light, it may flicker or not dim enough for you. Follow the Lutron directions about how to "trim" the dimmer so that you can set the dimming range just right. You will only have to do this once when you put different brands of bulbs in; after that just leave it alone. Next, we want to make this work on the phone.

Lighting

First, we'll focus on the Lutron devices being controlled on your phone. In order to make this work, you need to buy a Lutron bridge that plugs into your home router. The reason you need one is that the Lutron switches (like many other Smart Home devices) do not speak the same wireless language that your smartphone does. Your smartphone connects to your network using WiFi, but the Lutron devices connect wirelessly using something called Clear Connect. The Lutron bridge speaks both. When you buy this, it's best to get it with one of the bundles that also includes a dimmer switch as it is a fair bit cheaper that way.

Again, follow the directions that come with the bridge which will instruct you to install the Lutron app on your phone. Follow all the steps in the app and in a few minutes, your bridge will be up and running. You only have to install the bridge once and then never touch it again.

You'll use the Lutron phone app to add each of the switches, lamp dimmers, and Pico remotes that you've installed. Use the new e-mail address that you created (see page 95) to register the app. Install each device one at a time and give them all names, assign them to rooms as per the instructions on the app. You can also play around and set schedules and I'd encourage you to explore it a bit but don't go crazy with scheduling and creating lighting scenes just yet, because there is a better way to do it when you start to include some of the other devices from other manufacturers. But at this point, using the Lutron app for the Lutron switches, you can operate them while inside the home on your home network as well as while you're away from home. We'll go into this in more detail after we install a few more things.

Next is the installation of the iDevices outdoor switches. Initially, do this indoors in clear view of your router. These devices are WiFi enabled and so there is no need to install a bridge to get them to work on your phone. Again, use the app that iDevices specifies to do the installation, and more than likely the devices will also need a firmware update, so do that too as instructed by the app. It may take two to three repeats of each device for them to get properly installed, but be patient and persistent. Once they are working with your phone, unplug and move them to where you want to use them outdoors. Since they are WiFi (2.4GHz), they are looking to make a wireless connection to your home router(s) in order to work. If it doesn't seem like they're working, take your phone and connect it to the 2.4GHz network in your home and move it to the same location as you are going to place the iDevices switch. Check that you are still on WiFi and run a speedtest from your phone to see if you have Internet connectivity. If your phone cannot keep the WiFi connection, there is a pretty good chance that the iDevices plug won't connect either. The only thing you can really do is to try to get a better line of sight (fewer walls) between it and the router or go back to Part A that talks about how to properly set up a home wireless network and how to extend it.

Because this is an on/off switch there should be no compatibility issues with any LED or other type of bulb. Using the iDevices app will allow you to control from both inside and outside the home network. A nice feature of the app is that you can look at the power draw (and therefore, cost) of operating the set of lights you are controlling.

Now, if you have an Apple TV installed and logged into your Apple ID, run the Apple Home app on your iPhone, you'll notice that both the Lutron and iDevices products show up automatically and are controllable through this one app making them look like they are from the same vendor. This is how I run the system day-to-day and you'll probably want to do the same.

In my experience, I have had some stability issues with the iDevices outdoor switches. It is fairly common to get a "No response" notation on the button in the Apple Home app rather than its on or off state. Most times, you can just hit the button on the app and it will tell you whether it's on or off and then it works properly. There were two occasions in the first month of use where two different units were just not showing up online and I had to unplug them and plug them back in. This is not the level of reliability that I think is acceptable for the price but it doesn't annoy me enough to return them at this point, as it still works greater than 95% of the time. The Lutron Devices have been 100% reliable. I do not have any of the iDevices outdoor switches in my new home because the outdoor plugs that I intend to use happened to be controlled by indoor light switches. I will just use a Lutron switch on those and treat them like indoor lighting.

Applications to Run the System

As mentioned earlier, you'll need to download and install whatever app the manufacturer recommends to install a given product. But it doesn't mean that you need all of these to run things on a day-to-day basis. And to make things more interesting, you may have observed that while using the iDevices app that not only are all of the iDevices switches showing, but you can also see and control all of the Lutron devices too. The converse, however is not true in that the Lutron app cannot see the iDevices products and cannot control them. As mentioned previously, if you are running the Apple Home app on your iPhone or iPad, you will also see all of the devices from both Lutron and iDevices.

So, what should you do and why? We'll start by going through the functionality of the apps one by one and then recommend the best way forward.

Lutron app

The Lutron app is really top notch and so self-explanatory, that you just need to follow the directions and then start to play with it a bit as you add more devices. I have dozens of in-wall and lamp dimmers, Pico remotes, and motorized blinds (also made by Lutron – see Chapter 16). The Pico remote is a hand held remote that is handy for lamp dimmers that are in hard to reach places like the night lamps beside the bed, and they are also used mounted in the wall plates for three-way lights. They are assigned to whatever lamps or lights you want using the Lutron app. I set one as an overall master remote to turn everything on and off all at once and keep it in the nightstand by the bed. It is also pretty obvious how to turn on and off lights and how to dim them using the Lutron app on the phone. You can do this both inside and outside the home.

You can also add scenes, grouping a set of lights set at a specific level. For example, you can easily create all-on or all-off scenes where a group of lights is turned on or off with one touch of a button. You can also set schedules for turning lights on and off at certain times, including sunrise and sunset times (which will change as the seasons change). Again, these are very easy and self-explanatory and I suggest you experiment and if you make a mistake, you can just delete a scene or schedule and start over.

Lutron also allows you to add certain other devices to control within the Lutron app. These include the Lutron Serena motorized blinds but also non-Lutron devices such as thermostats. It's important to note that if you add thermostats to the Lutron app (for example), only the basic thermostat functionality is available within it, and in this specific case is not available to add to scenes or schedules. So, is this a bad thing? Not really, and we'll see later that one of the complexities of all these apps talking to one another is to try to figure out which one is really the boss and how many apps you really need to run things day-to-day.

There is one limitation with the Lutron bridge that you may stumble upon. It was something that I ran across when I added a number of smart blinds and Pico remotes. Your Lutron bridge can handle a total of fifty devices before you have to get another bridge to add more. Each switch, dimmer, Pico remote and blind counts as one, so for my situation, I have a total of over sixty devices.

If that happens to you, get another bridge, create another account with Lutron (one per bridge) and assign your devices to one bridge or the other. It would be extremely awkward to have to flip back and forth between two Lutron accounts to operate this on a day-to-day basis, so using the Apple Home app is the simple way to go. In this case, all devices from both bridges just show up in the Home app and you would use it to set scenes and schedules on a day-to-day basis.

Alternatively, Lutron has a higher end professionally installed system called RadioRA 2 that is designed for larger homes if you want to go that route.

iDevices app

The iDevices app is needed to get the outdoor on/off switches into the system. As mentioned earlier, all of the Lutron devices show up automatically (but not the third-party devices that were added to the Lutron app like Sonos for music or a smart thermostat), so now it is *possible* to control all of the lighting devices from just one app, namely the iDevices app. It has roughly the same functionality with slightly different terminology, but before going much further, it is a good time to pause and catch our breath a bit.

Simple Set of Rules for Apps

Always use the app that comes with the device you bought to install or add new devices of that type.

Use the app that pulls in the most devices to control a wider set of products for day-to-day use (example: the Apple Home app).

If you have a very specialized device that is rather complex, chances are you'll have to use that vendor's app day-to-day even though the goal is to have fewer of them.

We now have two ways to set up groups of switches and set schedules. Which one should we use? And what happens if we use both and they create conflicting schedules? The short answer is that this is why you bought this book. Sometimes more choice is a good thing but the reality is that it is pretty easy to trip over your own feet with all these apps. Before simplifying this, there is one more thing to discuss.

Apple Home app

If you have an iPhone or iPad running IOS 10.1 or greater (approximately October 2016), there is an app called Home that is available to install in the App Store (search for "Home"). If you were to click it now, without any setup or configuration, all of the Lutron and iDevices products will show up and can be turned on and off and grouped together into scenes. In fact, the scenes you created in the other apps show through in the Apple app. This is what Apple HomeKit compatibility is all about. If all the devices you installed in your Smart Home were HomeKit compatible, then they would all be controllable from one place, namely the Apple Home app.

One more thing about the Apple Home app. If you do have a 4th generation or later Apple TV, it enables both the scheduling, remote access and automation capabilities of the Apple Home app. The only configuration on the Apple TV to make this work is to enable *two factor authentication.* The Apple Home app will prompt you if you need to do this and although it sounds intimidating, you have probably seen this before when you log on to a secure site and it sends you a text with a code to make sure it is you. Just follow the directions online about how to do that with the Apple TV.

If you are on the Apple train and you do all of those things, then you can now control all of the lighting devices on demand with one app, both inside and outside the home. That includes full functionality for dimming, setting schedules, and scenes for controlling multiple devices at the same time both Lutron and iDevices. Later, as more devices are added, you can control them as well from the Apple Home app if the devices are HomeKit compatible.

Back to an earlier question: what would happen if you set up scenes and schedules in all three apps at the same time? They would all be executed by each of the apps and you will probably never figure out what is going on. Using the example earlier, I use the Apple Home app to control all the Lutron and iDevices products and remove any scenes and schedules from the Lutron and iDevices app. If I didn't have an Apple TV, then the next choice would be to use the iDevices app since it controls both iDevices and Lutron. Keep in mind that more Smart Home devices are going to be added later and it is anticipated that things like thermostats, door locks, garage door openers, etc. are more likely to fall under the Apple Home hierarchy rather than either Lutron or iDevices, so that is why I am choosing to use the Apple Home app wherever possible.

Also, later we'll run through some examples of a specialized device, like an outdoor sprinkler controller, that may never make sense to pull into the Apple Home app. There are other vendors out there who also strive to make the app that sits at the top of the hierarchy (Wink, for example) and while you can theoretically pull in a sprinkler controller integration, the functionality is so watered down (pun intended) that it is effectively useless to do so. But don't worry about that now - it will become much clearer later.

Bottom Line - Lighting

What to Do

LED bulbs are the way to go due to their low power usage, non-toxic nature, dimmability and now, more reasonable prices. Make sure you choose dimmable vs. non-dimmable even at the slightly higher prices unless you are counting every penny.

Pick a wattage equivalent and bulb size that matches what you currently have. Choosing a light temperature of 2700K (soft white) is a good starting point if you're not sure what to do. Only buy a few to test them with your new dimmers and make sure they are easily returnable. Be patient. Once you find some that work, you are all set.

Also, with LED bulbs, higher wattage bulbs (over 60W) are quite a bit more expensive, so when replacing some 100W incandescent bulbs, I chose 60W equivalent LED bulbs and was quite pleased with the results.

I standardized my home with mostly Ecosmart bulbs from Home Depot because they are reasonably priced, there is a wide selection of different shapes and sizes, and there are plenty of Home Depot stores around. I also used Cree bulbs with success and experimented with Sylvania bulbs, but had to return them to Lowes due to a loud buzz when the lights were on at any level. I did have success with Utilitech (Lowes) and Satco (lighting stores and online).

If you want to experiment a bit, you can also try different light temperatures other than 2700K and see if you like them. 5000K bulbs will give you a broad daylight feel but will definitely not match the rest of your bulbs. I have mixed incandescent, CFL, and 2700K LED all in the same room and nobody notices the difference.

If you want to try color (red, blue etc.), pick up a few smart bulbs and see if you like them. Once you see the cost, you will likely agree that these are more of a novelty item as opposed to something that you would put all over the house. (Unless you're planning on turning your whole house into a dance hall!) Philips HUE bulbs are a good place to start experimenting.

For light switches, replacing them with the Lutron Caséta in-wall dimmer is a simple, solid, and elegant solution. If you have three-way or multi-way switches, pay the extra $5 and get the small remote (called Pico remote) that will mount in the wall and function like the second switch.

For lamps, the Lutron Caséta wall dimmer is a great solution. Again, if the dimmer is hard to access, there is a kit that includes a Pico remote for $5 extra. Remotes are easily repurposed and programmable to any or multiple dimmers.

For outdoor lights that are plugged into GFCI outlets, the iDevices outdoor switch worked but try to get them on sale and keep your eyes open for other models from other vendors.

Get the Lutron bridge so that all the Lutron devices can talk to your home network and therefore your smartphone. The Lutron bridge is also Apple HomeKit compatible that enables use of the Apple Home app.

The iDevices product is WiFi so no bridge is needed for that. Use the vendor specific apps to do the installation of each device. Once everything is installed, iPhone users will want to use the Apple Home app (requires a 4th Generation Apple TV to remotely run the system) to set up lighting scenes and program on and off times.

If you don't want to use the Apple app, the iDevices app will allow you to control both Lutron and iDevices from local and remote. (The Apple app is better in my opinion as is the Lutron app, but as of this writing, the Lutron app did not allow for control of the iDevices products). Keep in mind that of any aspect of the Smart Home, the app part of it will change the most so always be open to experiment a bit.

Budget

Budget about $4.00 per bulb for dimmable LEDs that are 60W equivalent or less. Non-dimmable LED are approaching $1.00 each but of course they won't work with dimmer switches.

Colored bulbs (Philips Hue) are about $50 each and also require a bridge (another $50), hence my rationale that these are really more of a novelty as opposed to something you would put in every light socket. There are also smart bulbs with speakers built in that start in the order of $30 and up. Again, you would have to experiment with these if you think this is something you would want.

Budget about $50-$60 for the Lutron Caséta in-wall dimmers and Pico remote control. The same pricing applies for the lamp dimmers. The Lutron Bridge is in the $80 range when purchased alone but also available in a kit along with one in-wall dimmer and a Pico Remote for about $100 (a $40 savings from buying in pieces). There is also a Pico Remote wall plate bracket for $5 that you will need for each instance of a three-way switch installation.

The iDevices outdoor switch is a bit pricier than the $50 per switch industry price point but is often on sale so it may be worth waiting for a deal on that.

The Lutron, iDevices, and Apple Home apps are all free and none of them charge a monthly fee to remotely access your devices inside the home. You will need to download them all to install their respective devices but only the Apple Home app is needed to run all of those devices since they are HomeKit compatible.

Result

It was a lot of work researching, testing and returning products, but since you now have the benefit of having that done for you, I would say that this is probably the most important part of the Smart Home design and definitely worth it all! Of course, you had work to do on your end, too. So, what do we get for all this?

Direct electricity bill savings by switching from incandescent bulbs to LED bulbs. If you have ten, 60W bulbs on for 5 hours a day and switch to LED, you can save at least $150 per year. If you have kids who leave a trail of light everywhere they go, you can double or triple that.

CFL (Compact Fluorescent Bulbs) bulbs take time to warm up and achieve full brightness and also happen to be toxic waste due to the small amounts of mercury used. LED bulbs are instant on and they're nontoxic.

Setting moods with dimmers not only saves more electricity but makes certain family members happy. (It can also help you get family members if you don't have any!)

Automated timing makes your home looked lived in whether you are there or not and you can see the status and change it when you are away.

Using your phone to control lights is very cool to show other people as well as being very handy more times than you would think.

The Lutron devices have been 100% reliable for me and iDevices have worked at least 95% of the time with occasional reboots needed. The Apple Home app and using the Apple TV as the remote gateway has been extremely reliable as well, with no issues to date.

Chapter 9 – Thermostats

I'm not sure many people thought there would be much of a market for a Smart Home thermostat but one group of people called Nest did, and they were later validated by building a great product and being acquired by Google for a few billion dollars. Hmm. Maybe there is something to it after all.

If you go back to one of the basic Smart Home goals of having a minimum number of apps to run the system, then logic would say that I would pick a HomeKit-enabled thermostat and it would just feed into the Apple Home app. That's not a bad plan, but it's not what I ended up doing the first time around. Maybe it was the $50 off sale on Nest Thermostats or maybe it was because a recent visit to a friend's house who had one made me a bit envious, but I decided to use the Nest thermostat and use the Nest app to run it. I made the decision to go with the Nest product first because of the reviews on Amazon and also because Nest, and therefore Google, are vying to be a key player in the Smart Home area. Given that there is no clear winner yet, I wanted to have a foot in both the Apple and Google Smart Home plans.

Even though I know next-to-nothing about thermostats or their wiring, the whole installation was very well illustrated and simple, even to the point of having a very cool looking screwdriver included in the box. Before buying any Smart thermostat, always check their web site for compatibility with your current model. Normally that means opening up your existing thermostat and taking a picture of the wires and comparing it with the choices on the web site.

I replaced a rectangular thermostat with a round one, so I was concerned that I would have to fill holes and do paint touchups which aren't difficult but always seem to be the last thing on my list of fun things to do. Luckily though, Nest includes an optional rectangular faceplate to cover up the spot where the old one was.

The Nest thermostat is WiFi enabled so there is no need to buy a separate bridge in order to get it working on your network. It offers a choice of 2.4GHz or 5GHz WiFi networks and, in keeping with my convention of putting low volume Smart Home traffic on the 2.4GHz network, this is how I connected it. You will need to download the Nest app to set it up and run it day-to-day. Since the Nest is not Apple HomeKit enabled, it does not show up in the Apple Home app. Nest does have a pretty extensive set of "Works with

Nest" partners so it is likely that you will have some other app that you can use to also control the Nest. For example, if you followed my lead and used Lutron products for lighting, the Lutron app can control Nest thermostats. But just because you can do something doesn't always mean that you should! I did import the Nest thermostat into the Lutron app but will choose not to do this moving forward for two reasons.

First, only a subset of the Nest thermostat functionality is available when using the Lutron app. As I pointed out before, this will be a common theme throughout the challenge of integrating Smart Home apps.

Second, if you recall, the Lutron app, while a nice design and easy to use, feeds the Apple Home app which is what I use on a day-to-day basis for lighting and other things (not the Lutron app). And even if you import the Nest functionality into Lutron, only the Lutron devices carry through into the Apple app. I had this moment of hopefulness that perhaps the Nest could also be managed with the Apple Home app using this method, but it was not to be.

The Nest app for thermostats (and smoke detectors - see the next chapter), operates both inside and outside the home with no monthly fees. It's also very easy to add family members so that you don't have to set up multiple accounts. You can also manage everything right at the thermostat itself by turning the outer ring and pressing on the center. Once again, nobody would need a manual to use this.

Having said all this about Nest, it turns out that we used the Nest app quite a bit to adjust the heat and as such it would be much more convenient to have that functionality inside the Apple Home app. As we moved into a new home and made these decisions all over again, the second time around I used the Ecobee 3 thermostat, which is Apple HomeKit enabled, and also supports multiple room temperature sensors and displays the outside temperature. This is one of those situations where choosing the Apple Home app route could have a large influence over which product is the right one for you.

Bottom Line - Thermostats

What to Do

Nest has really set the industry standard and makes an excellent product although it is not Apple HomeKit enabled. I first chose Nest and use the free Nest app that comes with it to manage the thermostat inside and outside the home. There are HomeKit enabled thermostats available from Honeywell, Ecobee and others, so if you want to stay true to HomeKit, there are a number of choices available. My next install was the Ecobee 3, which has a nice feature that includes the use of temperature sensors placed in other rooms to get a more accurate read on the average temperature of the whole house rather than just where the main thermostat is located. In the winter, this will keep the rest of the house warm even if you have a fireplace on blasting out heat in the same room as the thermostat.

Make sure you check the compatibility with your existing system before buying a smart thermostat, but it is designed to work with most furnace and air conditioning systems. Every Smart thermostat maker has a simple tool on their web page that walks you through how to check this.

Budget

Budget about $200 to $250 per thermostat. There are occasional sales and promotions from most vendors, and you can also look at rebates from your utility company as well.

Result

Any kind of product that lowers ongoing utility costs is a candidate for automation because in all likelihood, the efficiencies of the product will pay for itself over time in utility costs savings alone. This applies to lighting (electricity costs), thermostats (gas, oil, propane or electricity costs), and outdoor sprinkler systems (water costs).

Also, because it is so easy to use, we actually use it to set temperatures for different times of day and conserve by lowering the heat while we are out. My wife especially likes it on cold winter mornings where the heat goes on and warms everything up before popping out of bed. That would be her main reason for saying it is worth it.

On the other side, I underestimated how important HomeKit integration would be for our setup. Since we use the Apple Home app for lighting, door locks, blinds and a garage door opener, family members naturally gravitate to the Apple app even when wanting to turn up the heat. It turns out that we use the thermostat function quite a bit more than I would have thought, so unless Nest comes out with a HomeKit version (unlikely in my opinion), I am sticking with Ecobee.

Chapter 10 – Smoke Detectors

While considering the idea of putting a Smart Home book together a few years back, I am pretty sure that a connected smoke detector was the last thing on my mind. On the other hand, I did like the idea of not waking up in the middle of the night to silence a chirping smoke detector battery. Yes, I am admitting that I didn't change the batteries every year like you are supposed to.

Smart smoke detectors started to show up on the market and they also included carbon monoxide detection. The question is, do we bother with this or not? To me, a smoke detector falls into the category of having insurance. I hate to pay extra for them because most of the time you don't need it, but when you do need it, it can save your life.

As with thermostats, there are a couple of choices to make when deciding which product to buy. There are smoke detectors from First Alert that are HomeKit enabled and will work with the Apple Home app. There is also the Nest

Protect smoke detector that falls under the Nest part of Google that works with the same Nest app as the Nest thermostat.

I chose the Nest Protect mostly because of its online reviews and also since works with the same Nest app that I initially used for the thermostat. Since the smoke detector is something that I won't be interacting with on a day-to-day basis, I don't think it's as important to be integrated with the things that the Apple Home app is controlling. I am really more interested in being loudly wakened if I am in the house and there is smoke, and notified if I am not at home should one of them go off. Later, when we cover security systems, it will be more advantageous to tie into that system.

When you buy smoke detectors, it's important to know whether they are wired into the home's electrical wiring or if they are standalone and operate on battery only. The easiest way to check this is to remove one of your existing smoke detectors with a simple twist and it will be obvious if it is wired in or not. Every vendor has two different models and always choose the wired version if you can. It still has batteries for backup but these smoke detectors will last a lot longer than if it only runs on battery. Don't be afraid of the wiring either, even though it is 120V. Take all the same safety precautions used when working with wiring for your lighting. It is even easier than doing light switches and most often there is a single circuit breaker for all of the smoke detectors to shut off when you are rewiring for the new product.

Read all of the directions before installing. For example, it is much easier to do all the installing with the Nest app when all the smoke detectors are lined up on the counter rather than when they are physically installed. The whole process is very painless but there are a few tips to offer you.

The Nest smoke detector is connected using WiFi so have your WiFi password handy as you will need it for the first unit you install. Most often, you are replacing a round smoke detector which leaves a round mark on the ceiling depending on how long it has been up there. The Nest is square with rounded corners and doesn't cover up the round mark completely, so depending on the paint situation on the ceiling, you may want to do some touchups before mounting the Nest bracket. In my case, a damp cloth did the trick and since nobody else noticed the slight marks, I chalk it up as an esthetic success. Lastly, if you test the smoke and carbon monoxide alarms, you might want to wear earplugs and let the dog out first. They are amazingly loud.

Once they are installed and running, there isn't really much to do with them on a daily basis. You can monitor them from the Nest app (the same one that also has the Nest thermostat) and about the only thing you can do is play with the white ring light that acts as a motion sensing night light when it's dark. You can also check on the status of all aspects of each smoke detector, including the battery percentage, which will conveniently alert you by phone when they need replacing rather than waking you up chirping at 3am.

Although I did not choose the Nest Thermostat for my new home, I still installed the Nest Protect Smoke Detector mainly because it consistently has the best ratings. See Appendix 2 at the end of this book for tips on how to use online ratings to quickly assess the quality of each Smart Home product.

Bottom Line – Smoke Detectors

What to Do

There are at least two choices for Smart Home smoke detectors. First Alert makes one that is Apple HomeKit enabled and Nest makes one that can be managed by the same app that is used for the Nest Thermostat. I chose the Nest model mostly because I don't anticipate needing to use an app on a day-to-day basis to interact with the product.

Budget

Budget about $120 per smoke detector. It is surprising how many are needed even in a small home (one per bedroom, hallway and some on each floor) so when I went around and counted nine in total, the bill came to just over $1000. A normal smoke detector costs about $30-$50 so the incremental cost was about $400-$600. A typical three-bedroom home would still have five to six of them.

The Nest smoke detector has a lifespan of ten years and I replaced some old ones that had been in the home twenty years, so maybe they were dead anyway. There are no monthly fees to use the Nest app remotely to check on the status of the smoke detectors.

Result

For me, not having batteries chirping at me in the middle of the night, and being able to see if anything bad is happening when I am away, are enough reason to spend the extra money on this type of product. If you really want to see how it works, let the dog out and burn a piece of toast under one of the units. You'll be impressed with the warnings you get. I am certainly happy with the Nest product and don't think it is important to have that type of product as part of the Apple Home app since you don't interact with it on a day-to-day basis. Typically, an integration into the home alarm system makes more sense. Also, I have come to love the built-in night light that comes on when you enter a dark room.

Chapter 11 – Outdoor Sprinklers

This type of automation is for your outdoor watering system for lawns, trees, garden, etc., not your indoor fire sprinkler system to put out fires. You may or may not already have one of these sprinkler systems in place with an existing control box typically made by companies like RainBird. These are either mounted on the outside wall of your home or perhaps in the garage or other indoor location. If you don't have this type of system already, you can probably skip this chapter because there is a lot more involved installing this from scratch than simply replacing an older controller with a new smart controller.

If you simplify what is happening behind the scenes (or more accurately, buried underground) in a sprinkler system, it boils down to a fresh water source being split into several directions, more commonly known as zones, each with a control valve that can turn the flow of water on or off for that zone. If you follow the pipes after the valves, they physically spread out into different parts of your yard to cover a certain area for watering. For example, you may have one or more zones for the front lawns with popup sprayers, one or more for the back lawns, one for the garden that is on a drip system, one for trees, etc. The valves don't know or care what lies beyond since they only know that they are either on or off. It is up to the landscape designer to put the zones in the right places and not to have too many taps or sprayers that overrun the capacity of a valve being in the on position. These valves are often located near the control box, sometimes above ground or sometimes buried in the ground in protective landscape housings.

As you can imagine, setting up all that pipe and doing all the trenching and cleaning up is quite a big and expensive job, so this chapter is all about making the most of your existing system by replacing the sprinkler controller. Again, the controller's only real job is to turn the valves on and off at the right times so that your plants and grass get the right amount of water. The obvious question is: why take a perfectly good controller and replace it with one that is smart and connected? Here's a handful of reasons:

- Considering that a controller's only real job is to turn valves on and off, it's astounding just how complicated these can be to program. It is one of the pieces of gear that you probably need to adjust four times per year for seasonal changes and every time I had to do mine, I had to re-read the manual. If you are like some of the people in my neighborhood, you don't even bother with that and you are paying a landscaper to handle it, or you massively overwater things. An expensive proposition either way.

- If rain is forecast or it's raining when the sprinklers are set to run, it's a waste of water to let that cycle run. Smart controllers know the weather and will take care of that automatically, directly saving in water costs.

- Where we live we don't get snow, but there are nights that are below freezing. A smart controller will stop the sprinklers in freezing temperatures.

- Depending on your property size, the largest contributor to your water bill is landscape water. Mine varies from $80 per month in the winter (when there is minimal watering) to about $200 in the heat of the summer. We have also had water rationing during our recent drought in Northern California and we have to adjust for that too. With a smart controller, you can set your water cycles once without using a manual (it's that simple), and the system will automatically scale the amount of water based on the seasons.

- Anyone who has a sprinkler system also has repair parts because they always sprout leaks. To fix a system the old way, you have to turn on a zone at the controller, walk over and find the leak(s), run back and turn the zone off, go back and fix the leak, go back to the controller to turn it on again, walk back to where the leak was to make sure it is fixed and then run back to the controller and turn it off again. I so dreaded that dance that I had the leakiest system on the block. With a smart sprinkler controller, you can roam around the yard with your smartphone and turn on and off zones and do repairs on the spot.

What do you need to know to replace your existing sprinkler controller? First, figure out the number of zones you currently have. New systems are typically eight or sixteen zones so if you have eight zones or fewer, you can buy the less expensive eight-zone model but you'll need the sixteen-zone unit if you have between eight and sixteen zones. If you have exactly eight zones, you probably don't need to buy the sixteen-zone model to have spare capacity unless you know you are going to expand or redo your system which involves lots of digging for new pipes.

Next, these controllers are normally connected to your home network using WiFi so take your smartphone to the location of your existing sprinkler controller, put it on your 2.4GHz WiFi network and perform a speedtest to make sure that you have connectivity. Do this before purchasing a new unit. The only way to remedy a situation of no connectivity is adjusting or extending your wireless network to include this spot as a coverage area. Go back and re-read the chapter on setting up your home WiFi network if you are not sure how to do this. You will not be able to move the location of the sprinkler controller easily since all the wires from each of the valves controlling the flow of water to each zone all come back to exactly where your current sprinkler controller is installed.

The only other consideration is whether the controller is located indoors or outside in the elements. If it is located outside, be sure to get the outdoor enclosure to match the new controller unit that you purchase.

Considering the controller, there are a number of vendors in this space, namely Rachio, GreenIQ, Skydrop, and Rainbird. I chose the Generation 2 Rachio unit back in April of 2016 when it first came out. Rachio was one of the first smart sprinkler controllers on the market and has excellent reviews. It's available at most major hardware retail outlets. Rachio is a US based company with local support and very responsive to questions or issues that you may have. This is something that you can easily install yourself with a few helpful tips below.

Depending on the physical size of your previous controller, you may need some paint touchups for the house once you remove the old unit, since the new one will likely be a different size.

If you can decipher your current watering schedule from the existing system, write down the times and dates for watering in each zone so that you have a starting point. Remember though that just because it is running this way now, doesn't mean it's correct. If you have dead grass or trees you may need to turn it up. If water gushes through your toes when you walk across the lawn every day, you are overwatering.

You will need to turn off the circuit breaker before removing the old controller. The wiring may seem intimidating, but Rachio has excellent directions so read them carefully and you shouldn't have any issues. For most systems, there are three wires for the main power, one common ground wire for all of the sprinkler valves, and one wire for each valve. It's not really that big a deal if you mix up the zones moving from the old system to the new system because you are going to be naming the new zones instead of remembering numbers.

From then on, setup is either on the Rachio app on your smartphone or from the Rachio web site. Both use the same account and it will be self-explanatory how to set it all up. I suggest you name all your zones with something meaningful and if you were able to record your existing watering times, input those as a starting point. Remember that if you have wide variations in watering times with the seasons, pick watering times that are appropriate for whatever today's date is. When you set up a schedule use the *smart cycle* and *weather intelligence* features. This is what makes the system so great along with the ease of use from your phone and computer. I also enabled notifications on my phone so that I am able to see when watering occurred and just keep tabs on things, especially in the early days when I was getting used to the system.

None of the systems are Apple HomeKit compatible so this function of controlling sprinklers pretty much has to stand alone in terms of day-to-day usage. Rachio does have a Nest integration that you can try out although it doesn't really do anything useful for me. Also, if you use Wink, you can integrate with Rachio as well, but you only get a subset of functionality. There is no need for any type of bridge to connect Rachio to your network since it uses WiFi, which your home network already supports.

Bottom Line - Outdoor Sprinklers

What to Do

I had a ten-zone watering system and replaced an overly complicated Rain Bird controller with a sixteen zone Rachio Generation 2 WiFi connected outdoor unit and installed it myself quite easily using Rachio's instructions having never set eyes inside one of these before. The iPhone app is excellent as is the web interface and all of the weather sensing features work (skipping on rainy days, not watering when it is below freezing, auto adjusting run times for seasonal changes, etc.) It works using your 2.4GHz WiFi so you have to make sure that you have coverage where the unit is going to be installed. It's very simple to test the Rachio system using your smartphone just by walking around the yard and turning the different zones on and off and making sure it works without any leaks or gushers.

Budget

Budget between $200 to $250 for the larger sixteen zone models – about $50 less if you only need eight zones. Outdoor enclosures run in the $30 range and are available for the controllers that require them. There are no monthly fees to use the app or web interface from inside or outside your home.

Result

This was one of the first things I bought when I started moving towards Smart Home technologies. Water is only going to get more expensive over time and seeing it pour down the street drains is not only akin to burning dollar bills, it is a waste of our precious resources. Even if I didn't save a penny in water costs or have a landscaper set up my watering, it is worth it just for the ease of use and finally being able to take simple control of my outdoor watering system.

Chapter 12 – Door Locks

The door locks being referred to in this chapter are your home's deadbolt locks on exterior doors and not the inside doors like the ones to the bathroom. Of course, if you feel you need a deadbolt on your bathroom door, there is nothing stopping you! (Some people *really* cherish their privacy!) A regular deadbolt has a manual turn piece on the inside and opens with a key from the outside. Newer smart deadbolts can be locked and unlocked manually on the inside but have several options to open from the outside. Among these are using a key, a security code entered on a keypad, and an electronic key fob. You can even use your phone to open the door with certain brands! (Hint: you want this!)

Some locks have several of these possibilities and some have only a few. The question is, what do you need and what are the considerations when trying to find the right one for you?

The first thing to do is find out what brand you already have installed. If you keep the same brand when moving to a smart lock, it's probable that you will have a simple physical installation because all the holes and cutouts line up. Also, some doors have the deadbolt integrated with the door handle. I had this on one of my doors, and rather than an elaborate effort to patch holes and touch up paint, I chose to leave that door alone for now and focus on the ones that have a physically separate deadbolt.

Going back to my earlier ease-of-use requirements, I still want to be able to use a key to get in, which would be necessary should the batteries die or the motor fail for any reason. I also like the numbered keypad so that I can assign codes to guests or workers who may need temporary codes, or for the kids to use. Since I have an iPhone and use HomeKit and Siri, I also looked for something that is Apple HomeKit compatible. I specifically don't want someone to be able to just touch the lock and open it since phones can be lost and it would be pretty easy for someone to unlock the door that way just by having your phone in their possession.

There are dozens of brands of deadbolt manufacturers but three that I will mention are Kwikset, Schlage, and August. Kwikset and Schlage both make smart locks with the Kwikset Premis and Schlage Sense being HomeKit compatible. August also adapts onto an existing deadbolt by installing a different part on the inside of the door that you can turn manually, has the motor and batteries to turn the lock remotely, and is also HomeKit enabled. Since August uses your existing exterior key deadbolt, there would not be a touch keypad for locking and unlocking from the outside but you get to keep the same key that you used before. Kwikset also has a simple re-key feature that lets you use your old key as well and you can do it yourself in about five seconds.

I chose the Schlage Sense Deadbolt in the first house since I already had Schlage locks, and Kwikset Premis in the new one. They are both HomeKit enabled, and I have the newer generation 4 Apple TV (to be able to control it remotely). Both have key entry and one-touch locking from the outside, a programmable keypad to unlock from the outside (don't use your phone number as your secret code!), and can also be unlocked using the vendor's app or the Apple Home app. Once again, I only use the vendor app for installation, checking on battery life, and updating firmware on the lock. The Apple Home app (or Siri) is more convenient to use on a day-to-day basis and it also makes it easy to include the lock as part of a scene like a *good night* scene where all the lights go out and the door locks.

The reason for the Apple TV is that this is how the Schlage and Kwikset models I chose, connect to the network. They both use Bluetooth Low Energy (BTLE) to connect, which means that it has to be forty feet or less from the Apple TV. Another reason for buying these locks at a local hardware store: it is either going to work or it isn't, and if it doesn't, you somehow have to bring the Apple TV closer because the door is staying where it is. Bluetooth extenders also exist and that may be worth a try but I have not used them myself. If it turns out to be impossible, luckily you kept your receipt because you'll need to return them.

From a physical installation perspective, as long as your current deadbolt opens and closes without having to force the key or jiggle the door, the motorized one will work just fine. The physical deadbolt that installs in the door and the strike-plate that installs in the wall matched up perfectly with my old same-brand unit, so that part was easy. This does involve some screwdriver work so allocate about 30-45 minutes to install your first one.

The Schlage and Kwikset directions are pretty straight forward, but read them in their entirety before starting as there is a temptation to jump ahead. Installation is done using the vendor app on your phone, which provides step by step instructions. Once set up, this model will automatically show up in the Apple Home app and be ready to use with that app as well. There are some caveats to be aware of:

On an iPhone, by default, with no password, there is a control panel that can be accessed by swiping up from the bottom of the screen that allows for shortcuts to several functions (airplane mode, calculator, flashlight, etc.) but also HomeKit buttons for lights, locks, or whatever you have as Favorites in the Home app. Only nine of the favorite home icons are there, but if one of them is the door lock icon, it means that without putting in your phone password, you can unlock the door. This is very convenient but not very secure. There are two ways around this: In IOS 10 or 11, go into the home app, find the door lock button, click on details and uncheck "Include in favorites". It will take the button off the Home tab in the home app and the control panel, but it will still be available in the Rooms tab in the app itself. The other way, in IOS 10, is to go into the iPhone settings, go to Control Center and uncheck the "access on lock screen" setting. This means that you won't be able to swipe up at all when your iPhone is locked. More secure, but less convenient. In IOS 11, it is much cleaner because you can configure what items are in the control panel so you can remove the Home App by customizing the controls in the Control Center settings and still swipe up with the lock screen on for other functions.

With both models, the only way to access the lock remotely (like checking to see if it is locked after you left on a trip), is by using Apple TV as a connection point into the network. If you don't plan on using Apple HomeKit, you will not have remote access to the lock, only when you are close and within Bluetooth range. Instead, both Kwikset and Schlage have different models that uses Z-Wave for remote access. Read Appendix 1 to understand what this means and what you would need to make it work.

By default, the app sends you a phone notification every time the door is locked or unlocked whether manually, through the app, or touchpad. This is really cool at first, but then you'll probably want to turn off the notifications so you don't get them every seven minutes.

Bottom Line - Door Locks

What to Do

Automating the deadbolts on exterior doors can be done from a number of vendors, notably Schlage, Kwikset, and August. Most allow for keyed entry, number touchpad locking and unlocking, as well as using your smartphone app/voice control from local or remote. Some are Apple HomeKit compatible but carefully check the model names to get the right one if you want that compatibility.

It is often easier to change out an existing lock with one of the same brand so that all of the holes and cutouts line up and the physical installation challenges are minimized. I replaced a manual Schlage lock with the Schlage Sense which is Apple HomeKit enabled meaning I can use Siri to lock and unlock it as well as the Apple Home app. The newer house replaces a Kwikset model so I used a Kwikset Premis HomeKit compatible lock.

Budget

Budget between $200 - $250 for each smart lock. There is no monthly fee to use the app from inside or outside the home. Using it outside the home does require an Apple TV as part of the Apple HomeKit system.

Result

If you can install it yourself, it's handy to have a smart lock on your main entry door. It's nice to be able to go out for a walk or bike ride without having to bring keys along. It's also handy to be able to warm up the car while waiting for family members to join me without having to shut the car off to lock the door with the key. Also, it is always reassuring to know the current state of your door lock when you are away. In the event of emergency, a trusted neighbor could be let in with the touch of your phone. If you have a worker coming to the house, you can let them in without being home. Both have been reliable and I haven't had any issues or unexpected things happen.

Chapter 13 – Garage Door Opener

There are two fundamental approaches to being able to open and close your garage door locally and remotely from your smartphone. The first one is to replace your existing garage door opener, which means the motor, with one that is Smart Home enabled. The second approach, and less expensive one, is to get an adapter that works with your existing garage door opener, allowing you to use both a smartphone app or your existing garage door remotes. For the purposes of this chapter, I will focus on the adapter style. Of course, if you are building a new home or replacing your garage door opener, you would choose the former and just pick a motor that is Smart Home enabled.

There aren't that many systems in the market, so we'll use the Chamberlain MyQ Garage system as our example. Chamberlain (aka LiftMaster and Craftsman) has a few different products to choose from, mostly determined by your starting point. So, job one is to go into your garage and figure out the brand and model of your current garage door opener. Look specifically for the "MyQ" logo or a "WiFi" symbol, as those are the main determining factors as to what product you will need. Your best bet is to then go to the Chamberlain web site under smartphone control products and run the MyQ compatibility tool to determine what type of model you should get. The first question asks you if you have an existing Chamberlain model, so remember to answer yes even if it is labelled LiftMaster or Craftsman, since they are all the same company.

Essentially, the older the model you have, the more expensive the upgrade will be. If you have a very old model, or if you're starting from scratch, a new garage door opener sells for approximately $250 before installation costs.

Using the adapter approach, there is typically a main unit needing AC power that mounts on the ceiling, near one of your garage door motors. This unit requires WiFi connectivity to your home network so the first job before buying one of these is to get a ladder, bring your smartphone to where you would install the unit and run a speed test on your 2.4 GHz WiFi network. If you did your network correctly as detailed at the beginning of the book, you will be fine to proceed. If not, go back and read Chapter 2 to revisit this topic and make any necessary corrections to your network.

If your garage door opener does not have MyQ capability, then you will be directed to a product that includes both a main unit and door sensors. The main unit talks with the sensor mounted on the garage door so that it can tell whether the door is open or closed. Essentially the main unit

(Chamberlain in this case) is signaled through your app and over your home network to send out the same remote-control signals that your car remote would use to open or close the door. This means you can still use your existing car remote if you want, as well as the doorbell buttons that are often mounted inside the small door into the garage. If you want to add a second garage door to the system, you just need an additional sensor on the second door plus programming it for its unique set of trigger codes.

In my case, I happened to have a LiftMaster garage door opener that is MyQ enabled. I want to use the system day-to-day using the Apple Home App so I needed a HomeKit enabled version of the Chamberlain MyQ Home Bridge. Fortunately, Chamberlain just released such a product in September of 2017 so I was able to proceed with this installation.

The MyQ Home Bridge screws into the ceiling near the garage door motor and plugs into the other half of the AC Power outlet used by the motor. It is connected to your Smart Home using your 2.4GHz WiFi network and then will talk the "MyQ" language to nearby Chamberlain garage door openers and accessories. Download the Chamberlain MyQ app and use that to install the bridge. With the bridge installed, you might think you are ready to raise and lower the door, but there is one more step to do.

Remember that the bridge only acts as a conduit between your smartphone and the opener, so the opener (motor) itself needs to be added in the app. It was not an obvious step, but by navigating to the "Places" section on the app you should see your MyQ bridge that you just installed, so select it and hit the "+" button on the top right. Then, click on the MyQ again (under MyQ Places) and then choose to add a Garage Door opener. You will then have to press a button on the opener (the motor) as described in the app, so have a ladder handy and the car out of the way. Once you have the opener installed, you are ready to impress family and friends by lowering and raising the garage door with the Chamberlain app.

If you did the HomeKit part of the installation when you installed the bridge (and you should), then both the bridge and the garage door opener will show up in the Apple Home app. The bridge icon is not used day-to-day so I normally uncheck the "include in favorites" button. Ask Siri to open or close the garage door. Create schedules that automatically close the door before you go to bed to ensure that it is closed at night.

The Chamberlain MyQ home bridge costs about $50 - $60 so if you were lucky enough to have a MyQ enabled opener, then this is a very cost-effective way to bring your Garage Door into the Smart Home world. And if you have multiple garage door openers, the same bridge will work for all of your openers.

Bottom Line – Garage Door Opener

What to Do

Automated garage door openers are available as add-ons for most existing openers or as a new motor that replaces the one you currently have. The main vendor is Chamberlain (aka LiftMaster or Craftsman). The Chamberlain MyQ Garage product is the one to look at to work with an existing garage door opener. The exact product to buy will depend on your existing model. The Chamberlain website will guide you in detail, but if you have an opener (the motor mounted on the ceiling) that has the MyQ logo on it, then you can use the less expensive MyQ Home Bridge. If your motor is a generic model or older, Chamberlain also has adapters for those types of doors.

I used the MyQ Internet Gateway (sometimes called MyQ Home Bridge) with our existing MyQ garage door opener. As of September 2017, this is Apple HomeKit enabled so it will integrate into the Apple Home app.

Budget

Set aside between $50 and $250 for a single garage door opener application. The amount you spend is largely determined by your existing model.

Result

This is a simple installation and very useful day-to-day. The HomeKit compatible bridge product works with the existing MyQ opener and is nicely integrated with all the other HomeKit compatible products.

Chapter 14 – Pool Equipment

This chapter only applies if you already have a swimming pool or if you are thinking about getting one. If you don't have a pool yet but are looking into it, there are a few choices to make when it comes to controlling the pumps, fill lines, spa, heater etc. I will also point out here that when it comes to pool equipment, using the terminology "Do It Yourself" is a bit of a stretch. These systems are almost always made for pool guys to setup so if you are anticipating making any changes, get your pool guy involved. He/she will probably have to do the install or make the changes.

The most manual method of pool control has all the controls right outside next to pool equipment. All the valves are manual, the pump is on or off and can be put on a timer that you'd manually adjust for the various seasons by walking out to the pool equipment. This type of setup is the least expensive and really only appropriate for the simplest of pools where there is no heater, solar, spa, or other changing water features. Again, your pool guy will be able to tell you what you'd need to automate a system like this. It would be extensive because you'd likely have to add basic computer control of all the functions (pump, valves etc.) and that could get pricey.

The Professor's situation started from a pool built in about 2005 that had a Jandy Aqualink RS control system with a remote panel that was physically wired from the pool equipment to a location in the kitchen. This was where all the programming for the pool equipment was done. We were fortunate when this was built that it was possible to physically install this wire from the pool, but it did take a pretty skinny guy who wasn't claustrophobic to crawl under the house to do it. If we had a concrete slab, I'm not even sure how they would have done it. The keypad is functional but it's not intuitive to program and although I always manage to figure it out, my family won't touch it.

But now, there *is* a better way. Jandy has an upgrade to the pool controller called iAqualink 2.0 that removes the old computer outdoors at the pool equipment and puts a new one in along with a WiFi Pod that is the pool equipment's link back to your home network. It uses 2.4 GHz WiFi, so again, using your phone at that location, connect to your 2.4 GHz WiFi and do a speedtest to determine if you have connectivity before making any purchases. Once the

> Your WiFi network can extend outside the home to connect with your pool equipment and other outdoor automation.

new board is installed and connected to your WiFi network, programming is done using a web interface typically on a larger screen like a laptop or iPad. The pool guy will do most of this and get your settings moved over to the new system, too. There is also a smartphone app called iAqualink that you'll need to download onto your phone and this will be used day-to-day if you need to turn the pool on or off, or switch to the spa. It replaces the controller that is wired onto the wall that you used to use. Our old controller is still there, however, and it's your choice whether you leave it or remove it and go exclusively with the phone.

This upgrade doesn't change any of the features that you previously had, it only changes the device you use to do the programming. I will say that the web interface is much easier to navigate, but the terminology is still in pool-guy language so you may have to play around a bit to figure out the right changes. The phone app works both when you are on your local network and when you are remote, so if you are thinking of jumping in the spa when you get home from work and want to fire it up before leaving, now you can do that. I found it handy to use when the pump went on at night for freeze protection on those chilly winter nights. I was able to turn the pump off during the day on its normal cycle to save on electricity. The iAqualink phone app doesn't offer any advanced functionality (as of late 2017) like notifications or any different programming choices, which is disappointing but it works as advertised in terms of being able to control all of the functions from my phone or on the web that I could only previously do from the kitchen.

Jandy isn't the only manufacturer of pool equipment control, so if you have another brand, now is the time to know your pool guy and see if he/she knows of a migration for the equipment that you have. Other major players are Hayward and Pentair.

In our new home, we are using the Pentair product line and the Screenlogic2 system that can be accessed on computer, smartphone, or even Apple Watch. It works a little differently than the Jandy system in that the wireless pod mounted by the pool equipment does NOT use WiFi to connect back to your home network. This means that you don't need to do the WiFi test at the pool equipment but something different instead. Pentair uses their own wireless technology to connect to a small antenna and a "protocol adapter" that will physically be installed near your home router. The protocol adapter plugs into one of the Ethernet ports on the router to connect the Pentair system to your network.

At press time, the system was not yet up and running so updates with full details will appear on the smarthomeprofessor web site.

Bottom Line - Pool Equipment

What to Do

Step one is to get your pool guy involved to find out whether it is an easy transition from the pool controller you have, to one that can be controlled by the smartphone. Jandy makes the iAqualink 2.0 system which was a board swap and reprogram operation for me. (actually the pool guy with me looking over his shoulder) If you are putting in a new pool, it is much easier since you need some kind of pool controller anyway. Other popular brands are the Pentair Screenlogic2 and the Hayward OmniLogic. The brand you choose will likely be determined by the type of equipment you already have, as that is the least expensive way to do the transition. For the new pool install, we used the Pentair Screenlogic2 system.

Budget

The Jandy iAqualink 2.0 upgrade kit was selling for about $600 on Amazon and my pool guy charged $180 to install it and set it up. Your cost may vary depending on what equipment you are starting with. Save the board that gets removed as there is a viable resale market on eBay so you may be able to pick up $100-$200 for the old controller board if you do an upgrade. If you are upgrading a Hayward or Pentair system, call your pool guy as your pricing will always depend on the details of your existing setup.

Result

From a functionality perspective, the Jandy iAqualink2 does everything as advertised. Pool equipment is just plain expensive so I would have felt much better about the overall value if the price came in around $300 for the upgrade. For the new pool install that we are in the middle of, we are using Pentair equipment, so full updates are on www.smarthomeprofessor.com

Chapter 15 – Video Door Bell

Starting in 2012 the first of the Smart Home video doorbells started to arrive on the market. The idea is that the doorbell now has a camera, speaker, and microphone inside and is connected to your WiFi network. When someone rings the bell, your phone is notified and you can answer the door with one way video (you can see them) and two-way audio from wherever you are. The doorbells also have motion detection so you can capture package thieves, kids ringing and running, deliveries, etc. While sometimes included as part of an overall home security system, the doorbells are mostly marketed and sold as standalones in the $200 - $250 range. They can either replace your doorbell by using its existing wiring or there are battery powered versions if you don't have wires. As of late 2017, notable vendors are Ring, Skybell, and August.

One thing to note here is that all of the main players in the video doorbell space are startup companies and none of the products to date come from established players in the doorbell industry. This is not necessarily a negative thing, only that there are certain characteristics frequently observed from startups. For the most part, startups are often under great pressure to push products out to market fast to satisfy their investors. There is always a fine line between rushing a product to market and releasing a quality product. Even though the first version of the product has to be good enough to gain market traction, often the second or third generation of the product is the one that will take over the mainstream market and be the one that everyone wants for the long term.

If you are buying version one of a startup product, you are probably an early adopter of new technology, love tinkering, and don't mind doing regular upgrades of both hardware and software. If you just want something that works, don't mind letting others be first, then you might be inclined to wait for the next version of the product.

I say all this because choosing which video doorbell to buy gave me great heartache. Roughly, from a functionality perspective they are comparable in terms of advertised capabilities. I have an issue with Ring because in order to retrieve all of the stored video clips from rings and motion detection, they charge a monthly ($3) or yearly fee ($30) which goes against my criteria of not wanting to pay monthly fees for any of this technology. In looking at the reviews on Amazon, Ring certainly has many more reviews than their competitors indicating much higher sales and the higher rating of the three. (See Appendix 2.)

So, once again, I violated my own rules, this time about no monthly fees, and got the Ring Video Pro doorbell. I got the newer Pro version even though it was more expensive simply because it was their latest model and I don't want to live with the mistakes of the older models. It turns out that wiring for doorbells is way more complicated than I could have imagined. Combinations of mechanical chimes, electronic chimes, or in my case no chimes, and a bit of a re-wire job from an old intercom system, made this a more advanced type of installation.

The lesson here is that whichever model or brand you buy, only buy it at a retail location that accepts returns because there are reasonable odds that something in your doorbell world will be incompatible with these products, whether it be the wiring, physical installation, or just missed expectations. Some vendors have rather nasty return policies if you buy them directly online. I was a bit lucky and unlucky at the same time, in that my specific wiring scenario was not the normal way of doing things so I had to get a hold of Ring support to have them ship me the missing part which turned out to be a fuse and some wire all neatly packaged up. They did so free of charge and a few days later, I was all set to install the doorbell.

Before you even buy or unbox the doorbell, you will want to do the 2.4GHz and 5GHz WiFi speed test again with your phone from the exact location you plan on installing the doorbell. If you can't get the recommended bandwidth at that spot, your options are to move the doorbell, which is as unlikely as moving the door, or adjust your WiFi network so that location is covered. Remember that it will be more important to have a good uplink bandwidth since it is video captured by the doorbell that needs to find its way up to the Internet for storage. I measured about 5Mbps uplink bandwidth (my service is maxed out at 6) and I got acceptable video. If you are measuring less than 1 Mbps and you can't get it any higher, this product might not be for you.

Of all the Smart Home products, this one is probably the most intensive physical installation. Unless you want to guess about the voltage of the wires at your doorbell (most use 24 Volts), you will need a voltmeter and know how to use it. Also, a little bit of creativity is required for the physical installation of the doorbell on the outside of the house. Although this wiring challenge might scare you into buying and running a battery-only doorbell, I'd recommend that only as a last resort. Batteries do not fare well in cold weather and some functions such as live view may not function the same as with a wired unit. If you choose Ring, follow the instructions very closely knowing that the Ring and Ring Pro have vastly different installation and wiring instructions. The documentation is good but quite often they mix the two units up which makes things confusing. I suspect this will get better over time. The rest is set up using the Ring app on the phone and is pretty straightforward. When the doorbell rings, the person ringing will hear a sound right at the doorbell so they know that they have pressed the button properly. Also, you will get a notification on your phone and anyone else whom you have invited, in my case, my wife's phone. If you wired it the normal way to your old doorbell chime, you will also hear that indoors as well. In my case, I didn't have a doorbell chime, so I bought the Ring Chime that plugs in to an outlet and connects with your WiFi network and is triggered by the ringing of the doorbell. It is also installed using the Ring app and works okay for both motion detection and ringing of the bell.

Reluctantly, I also purchased the $30 per year video cloud storage, where every ring or motion detection is stored by Ring for thirty days for later inspection by you using the Ring app. If you didn't get this option, you would only be able to do live views of someone ringing the bell or moving around the area but nothing stored to prove to the police that someone stole your package.

Skybell does not charge for cloud storage so there are other options if you feel more strongly than I do about not paying for ongoing usage of the product. Realistically you need the storage of events since most times you won't be available to respond to the notification on your phone. It is configurable, but every time there is movement or a ring of the bell, this event is recorded. There are settings to create your "motion zone" where motion will be detected and this has worked well for me with only a few false positives when it is very windy and a nearby tree moves. Our rather large cat thankfully does not trigger it when he takes his perch on our welcome mat. If your front door is really close to the road, you might have to adjust the sensitivity and trigger zones to make it less sensitive.

The Ring Pro camera leaves a bit to be desired in terms of actually being able to identify people, even in broad daylight. Even at its highest resolution, it is very difficult to capture clear images and zooming in is somewhat pixelated. Time will tell if this gets better or if somebody else comes along with a superior product.

Bottom Line - Video Door Bell

What to Do

There are a number of choices for replacing a standard doorbell with a video doorbell. The initial set of products to date have come from startup companies so remember that often the first-generation products are the ones you want your neighbor to try first. If at all possible, use the wired version of the doorbell and remember that the point of the product is to collect video, which needs a good WiFi network uplink connection from the doorbell location. Many of the vendors charge an ongoing fee for storing video clips of motion and doorbell rings. I am not a fan of paying this but I did it anyway with the Ring Video Doorbell Pro that I bought. The installation is a bit more involved than others and deals with low voltage wiring (typically 24V), so you probably need a voltmeter and know how to use it to tackle this install yourself. If you don't connect this to an existing doorbell chime, you will probably want to get the Ring Chime so people inside are alerted to movement and doorbell rings.

Budget

You should plan on spending between $250 to $300 total for these products assuming you install them yourself. Some have an annual fee for video storage on the order of $30 per year.

Result

I was a little unsure at first whether this would be a good spend, so far it has been mostly neutral to positive. There are an awful lot of motion notifications since we exit the front door frequently when walking the dog, but it does no harm and it just means we have a lot of recordings. The app has been stable but the recording quality is so low that you can only see that *someone* is there, not who they are in detail. You get full color recordings when it's light enough out and black and white even when it's pitch black.

Early on, I had some issues with videos being recorded as all black and I was told that the WiFi signal wasn't good enough. This led me back to the chapter on extending a WiFi network to add another small router to boost the signal to where the doorbell is located. Thankfully, this worked and as mentioned earlier, I found a spouse-approved place to tuck the new router unit away inside a grandfather clock.

Did I get one of these for the new house? The answer is not yet. I am still inclined to wait until the overall quality gets a bit better before investing in this again. It is certainly useful for people whose home is empty most of the time and need to respond to people at the door.

Chapter 16 – Motorized Window Blinds

Window coverings in the form of pleated shades or roller shades are candidates for home automation, allowing you to automate and control the ambiance in each room. Whether you want the blinds down at night for privacy, for shade on hot summer days on sun-facing windows, or if the window is in a hard to reach place, this type of solution may be right for you. Because these types of blinds are controlled with your phone, with voice commands, or with the vendor supplied remote controls, it means that they have a small motor to move the blinds up and down which, of course, means they also need power. In my home, the only real option is to use the battery power option since we don't have outlets near the tops of the windows. Motorized blinds are expensive so pay close attention to the example costs in the Bottom Line section at the end of this chapter.

Window blinds, like lighting, are typically things that you would use on a daily basis, so it makes sense to see if there is an opportunity to integrate the app you are already using for lighting to also schedule the blinds. This would steer me in the direction of two options: using the same vendor you are using for lighting or second, using something that is HomeKit compatible if you have chosen to use the Apple Home app.

There are more than a few vendors that have viable products for Smart Home blinds. Established blind vendors like Bali and Hunter Douglas both have motorized solutions with in-room control units as well as their own apps. Another solution is called Serena shades, which is a product of Lutron, the same Lutron that makes the Caséta Wireless lighting discussed in detail in the lighting section. This means that if you have gone the Lutron route for lighting, you can just add the Serena shades using the same Lutron app you're already using and the same Lutron bridge you installed for the lighting. You can also easily program the Pico remotes to control one or more blinds along with lights using the Lutron app.

Earlier, we discussed whether to use the Lutron app or the Apple Home app to control your home lighting and setting of all the schedules and groupings. If you chose the Apple Home app, the great news is that the Serena shades are also HomeKit compatible, so when you start adding them, they will automatically show up in the Apple Home app as well as the Lutron app. This also means that you can use Siri voice control on your Apple devices as well as integration to Amazon's Alexa should you enjoy barking out commands and seeing things move. For example, at night, I just say "Hey Siri, good night," and she dutifully closes all the blinds, turns off all the lights, and makes sure all the doors are locked. A luxury to be sure, but one that has quickly been taken for granted.

In our first house, we had fairly simple window coverings with neutral color pleated shades, some having room darkening and some just light filtering. We also had more than forty windows, so when I calculated the cost of a basic fabric (using a super fancy fabric can easily double the cost), my total cost for doing motorized blinds would have been about $14,000 - $16,000 which is about triple what I spent on everything else combined. For comparison purposes, a basic Levelor blind that you can get from Home Depot would cost about $3,000 to $4,000 to do the whole house. So, this Smart Home Professor also likes to be realistic and decided that in that house we would be pulling on strings to open and close blinds.

The new house has only about twenty windows in total, so we did end up putting motorized shades on all of them. It was still pricy but somehow, I felt better about it when the neighbor started telling me about the window covering consultant they hired to do designer coverings.

The serenashades.com web site is excellent and self-explanatory for all the different kinds of mountings, fabrics, and other options. Even though we use the Apple Home app and incorporate scenes and opening-and-closing schedules into this new design, we also made it possible to open and close them using a wall switch in each room. This is easily done by ordering the Lutron Pico remotes and installing them behind a wall plate anywhere on the wall. In the kitchen, for example, we have three windows that will all likely be opened or closed at the same time, so we just need one remote to program and control all three at once. In other rooms, we chose to go with one remote per blind.

We ordered the battery-operated version, which I suspect is what the vast majority of people do simply because there is no easy way to wire these in. Changing batteries is easy without having to remove the blind. Self-installation is simple, yet time consuming, so invest in an electric screwdriver.

Bottom Line – Motorized Window Blinds

What to Do

Installing motorized blinds is an expensive undertaking but if you chose to do it, I would pick something that uses the same apps that you use to control lighting, since the two are somewhat linked both in function and frequency of use. I chose Serena shades from Lutron due to its integration with many of my lighting choices and its Apple HomeKit compatibility. This is an easy method for combining lighting and blinds into the same schedules and use voice control. If you chose Lutron Caséta products for lighting, the same bridge is used for communicating with the blinds.

Budget

There are a lot of variables, not the least of which is the fabric type, that have a huge impact on the overall cost. For purposes of comparison, I chose the window right in front of me which is 70" wide and 40" high, inside mount.

The battery powered Serena blind, with the lowest end fabric priced at just over $500. A simple corded blind from Levelor and priced at Home Depot came in at $150 If you have a keen eye for design and want to upgrade the fabric, it is not difficult to double these prices. The best way for you to see if this is an investment you want to make is to price your own windows online on the respective web sites.

Result

I did not do this in my first home due to the high cost and the large number of windows, but I did go ahead and buy a much smaller number for the house we just moved into. Because all the Lutron equipment is Apple HomeKit compatible, I use the Apple Home app to program all the blind and lighting automations as well as to control individual blinds. In addition, in each room, I installed a Pico remote on the wall near the blinds to be able to easily raise or lower the blinds without needing a smartphone. The remotes install anywhere and without wiring and look just like a light switch. They are easily programmable with the Lutron app so you can change their function whenever you choose.

This is a luxury, but if you are looking to replace or buy new blinds, it's definitely something worth considering. It would be difficult to go back to the days of tangled strings and kids yanking them so hard that they broke off and had to be replaced...

Chapter 17 – Home Security System

Home security systems have been around for a long time. Often, we receive ads in the mail from security companies offering to give you a bunch of equipment for free in return for a 2-3 year commitment to their monitoring service, usually in the neighborhood of $40 - $60 per month. Reading all the fine print is mind numbing and often the free package is not really free because of all the add-on costs.

Recent entrants to this market — your phone and cable providers — will also provide a complete solution for some sort of commitment and an equally complex set of terms and conditions. To muddy the waters further, some of these packages will include home automation devices like many of the ones that have been discussed in previous chapters in this part of the book.

What should be part of a home security system and what should you do on your own? There is no one-size-fits-all answer for this, but hopefully you will get some pointers here that will steer you in a good direction.

If you already have a security system

Traditional home security systems typically offer the following as standard features:

- Perimeter protection (sensors) for doors and windows
- An indoor siren alarm
- Indoor control pad to arm and disarm
- Monitoring at a central facility via a cellular connection
- Motion sensors
- Glass break sensors
- Other bells and whistles that you probably didn't need

Typically, the system is armed when you are inside for the night so that it will go off immediately in case any door or window is opened. When out of the house, the system arms on a delay through your main door entrances. If any of the perimeter security is breached, the alarm company is notified, they call you and if you don't give them the correct code or don't answer, the authorities are called.

This isn't very useful if the notification to the alarm company goes over a standard phone line or wired Internet connection since those are only a pair of wire cutters away from being disabled by even amateur bad guys. Now, it's pretty much standard that the connection back to the monitoring site is done over the cellular network. As noted before, you would pay your $50 per month for this over a two to three-year contract in return for a "free" install of the equipment. This type of system qualifies you for the home insurance discount which varies, but is typically in the 10-20% range.

What happens at the end of two to three years after all the equipment is paid for? Does the alarm company call you and offer you a lower monitoring price or a batch of new gear? Probably not. But if you call and tell them you want to cancel your service, you might find that magically, your monthly fee gets reduced to something in the order of $20 per month. Don't accept their first offer either. There are systems out there in the $15 per month range and they have to remain competitive. I bring this up because this is a viable strategy for handling your home security system if you already have a system in place and are happy with it. The only thing you might want to add on is the ability to control arm/disarm and receive alerts on your mobile device. Many of the existing systems will offer this upgrade so check and see the one-time cost of doing this as well as what the new monthly charge will be. Most of the other fancy features like video cameras and other Smart Home products are easily installed by you and don't need to be part of a system that just drives up your monthly cost.

If you have a relationship with a phone or cable company (and you probably do if you have Internet, a cell phone, or TV), you are likely to be offered up a so-called bundle package that will combine things like TV, Internet, and home security. Often this comes with an introductory pricing offer that resets to a much higher price after one or two years. Again, read the fine print on all these offers so you know your overall financial obligation. If you like your service provider and think you will stay with them for a while, this option may be appealing to you.

Starting with a new system

The other scenario is that you don't have any home security system in place, or want to replace your current system, and you want to do this yourself for a reasonable price. There are dozens of systems out there so it is always best to start with a list of what you really need. My list was:

- Door and window sensors for perimeter security
- Indoor siren and main control unit (these are often together in one unit)
- Indoor control pad to arm and disarm
- Connection to a central monitoring facility via cellular
- Motion sensors (if no large indoor pets)
- Glass break sensors
- Smartphone control in and out of the home
- Easy integration with other sensors

This is the same list as before with the addition of smartphone control and the integration with other sensors. There are always other options like signage, key fobs etc., that you can add on but the obvious missing thing is video cameras. That will be covered later in the chapter since they have their own unique challenges. Before sharing a couple of options with you, remember that no security system will make your home burglar proof. Your goal is to keep family members safe, maximize the likelihood the bad guys get caught or better yet, make your house look less attractive to break into.

At the old house, I already had a system with a traditional security company, so I chose to get the lower monitoring price and just live with what I have for the time being, including no control with my smartphone. There are a couple of systems that I did consider for the new house, which was a clean slate for security.

The first one is from a company called SimpliSafe. You buy the gear that you need from them, install it yourself, and then choose the monitoring plan that suits your needs. Tucked away in their website is a choice of a basic monitoring fee of $15 per month, but it goes up to $25 per month if you want to use the phone app. Since that is a requirement for us, the monthly fee would be $25 with no commitment period.

For equipment cost, we'll use an example of a moderate sized bungalow with three door entries and fifteen windows.

If you have a big dog like we do, motion sensors are not of much use but a few glass break sensors would make sense. If you price this out from SimpliSafe, the cost would come to about $500 not including tax. If you look at the reviews on Amazon, which are plentiful and very good overall, you will also hear complaints that the main siren is not very loud so you might want the optional louder siren for another $60. There is a system maximum of forty-one sensors so make sure you figure out what you need before buying this system. It's been around for over five years now and gets excellent reviews from customers and evaluation websites. If there is any negative, it's that the company has been slow to come out with new products and capabilities and that the system is closed so that you can't integrate it with other vendor's products. Of course, this can change so make sure you make good use of Amazon reviews and the vendor websites to get the latest.

The other system has not been around as long but also has great reviews on Amazon, is more modular and open to integrations like Nest and sensors for things like leak detection. The Abode system has free self-monitoring with a smartphone app and offers two levels of central monitoring, one that has a cellular backup for $96 per year, or full professional monitoring, including the cellular backup for $240 per year (they also offer monthly rates). The unique thing on the monitoring side is that you can choose to get professional monitoring a la carte in three or seven day increments should you only need it for that period of time. The cost of the same system with Abode is a bit more expensive and comes in at over $900. It is not exactly an apples-to-apples comparison though, as it also includes an indoor motion sensor with camera that you have to get but costs $115 if purchased separately. Abode is constantly adding new capabilities and does frequent updates on their website to keep you informed. If you also have Nest products, it is worth also checking out how those integrations work on the Abode website. For example, if your Nest Protect smoke detector goes off, it will trigger an alarm to the monitoring center who then call the fire department.

I chose the more expensive system from Abode, along with the annual monitoring that averages out to $20 per month. I like the smaller low-profile window sensors that I was able to *just* fit on all the windows and clear the blinds that are inside-mounted. Installation was easy and I would recommend that you use your computer to do the install and then your smartphone to run things day-to-day. Everything is configurable (like each sensor can be on a delay or not, make a chime or not, etc.) so it will take you some time to figure out what you want, but once you do, it's a straightforward process. I chose not to have each door/window make a chime when it was opened or closed, and to have the two main entry doors on a delay so we can enter and have sixty seconds to get to the keypad to disarm when we arrive home.

The keypad is an optional accessory which we don't use all that much, since we can do everything from our smartphones, but it's useful if you're having someone come in to house-sit when you're away and you just want to keep things simple for them. There is an extensive notifications function for both e-mail and smartphone that could use some ease-of-use makeover. For each account you create, you'll have to manually check each of about 50 or more boxes as to the type of notifications you want. Flexible, but time consuming. At least you only have to do it once per account.

Security cameras

Cameras in general can either be part of your security system or not. Some people use them for baby or pet monitors or for keeping an eye on the backyard pool to make sure everything is going okay. Others use them as part of the security system and take advantage of motion alerts to trigger notifications that can be sent to their alarm system. There is an integration of Nest cameras and the Abode security system, for example, that allows for this capability.

The important thing to know about cameras is that each camera is capable of sourcing a live video feed of differing qualities. This feed can either go nowhere if nobody is watching it, be sent to your smartphone if you want to watch it on demand, or stream its video to some storage facility either continuously or when motion is detected allowing for later retrieval. There are substantial ongoing cost factors to consider such as the amount of your Internet bandwidth the camera uses and video cloud storage costs. Even though it gets a little involved, it's worth your time to understand these tradeoffs. We'll start with the most intensive application from an overall cost and bandwidth perspective and work our way down to the least.

Constant streaming to the cloud

This model has each of your cameras on and recording 24/7 with all the video data going over WiFi to your router, and then using your Internet Connection to store the video in a Cloud service (a place on the Internet where stuff is stored) for later retrieval. This is the most expensive of all models and to illustrate this, we'll use the Nest camera as an example since they are kind enough to share all this information on their web site.

Each camera recording using its highest quality video will use between 0.45 to 1.2Mbps of your Internet uplink capacity and of course that same amount of your WiFi network in your home. If you recall the speedtest examples used earlier in the book, the uplink number is often the lower one, and I was measuring 6Mbps. So, a three pack of these cameras would use between 1.5 and 3.6 Mbps of my Internet uplink (more than 50%). Yes, that is a lot.

Continuing on, over the course of a month, a single camera will generate between 140GB to 380GB of data going out your Internet link, just for storing the video. Again, recall that many Internet providers are now metering usage on your home Internet connection and charging for overages.

My Internet connection is metered at 1024GB per month (counting data in and out) so again, three cameras would use between 420GB and 1140 GB per month. This is also a lot, and in fact could put me in a position of having to pay more for Internet service just to handle this load. By the way, the reason that there is variation in the data coming from the cameras is that the less motion, the lower the data rate. More motion tends towards the higher number.

Now to add one more component to this model, the video generated by the camera needs to be stored somewhere and that is not free. Nest has a service called Nest Aware that has a yearly subscription of either $100 for ten days of rolling video storage or $300 per year for thirty days of rolling storage. Per camera. Yes, up to $900 per year for three cameras, each having thirty days of rolling storage and playback. (Note that these figures may change so make sure to check the latest figures on the Nest web site)

As you can see, this can get very expensive very quickly and for this reason, here are a few other models that make sense depending on your application.

Triggered event video clips stored in the cloud

It turns out that most of the time, nothing is happening on the cameras so there is no point in storing a continuous stream. In this model, used by the majority of the video doorbell vendors including Ring which I used, thirty second clips are recorded for each motion event detected as well as a press of the doorbell button. These clips are dated and timed and available to playback later using the appropriate Phone app or via the web browser. The quantity depends on how many events occur but hitting your bandwidth limits or overall data usage does not factor into this model. There is typically a cost to store and retrieve this video that varies by vendor so make sure you read the fine print. Ring costs $30 per year for thirty days of rolling video clips - just enough to be annoying but not so much that I didn't buy it.

Constant Streaming, Local Storage, on-Demand Retrieval

This model is similar to the first one where each camera streams continuously to a storage device but that storage is in your home so there's no need for extra data to clog up your Internet connection. To review any video, an app, or web browser can review live or interesting segments either locally or remote to your house. In the case of remote viewing, your Internet connection would be used but only when you are watching. From a pure security perspective, this is not as secure as if the video was stored offsite since someone can steal the storage device from your home if they know what to look for. It is possible to set up a system like this in your home by using a Network Attached Storage (NAS) with some custom programming and many of my tech savvy friends have done this, but I haven't yet found a simple to use commercially available system that works like this.

Since this is how I would run the system in my home, I am postponing purchase of a proper camera system until this becomes available. I will provide timely updates on www.smarthomeprofessor.com on this topic.

Streaming on Demand Only

This model is quite simple and it can be done with the same cameras as the constant streaming to the cloud model, with the exception being that you are not paying for any storage of video in the cloud and you can connect to the camera on demand and watch live video. Only then is it streamed over your WiFi and to the Internet when you are not home. Despite my postponement of getting a proper camera system, to test this I got the Nest Outdoor camera and set it up in the garage so I could see what the cats were up to and to be able to check if the garage door was open. Admittedly this is a silly reason to buy a camera but hopefully you'll find a better application than mine.

Since we had already installed some Nest thermostats and smoke detectors, we used the same Nest app on our phone to do the install of the camera. Again, the installation is pretty straightforward using the directions that come in the box. I decided that I would try to use this on my 5GHz WiFi network since it uses a lot of bandwidth when streaming and I know that the 2.4GHz network already has a lot of devices. A quick speedtest using my phone from the desired location showed enough bandwidth to go ahead so using my existing

Nest app and account, I just added the camera to the app. I did *not* sign up for the Nest Aware expensive cloud storage so that I could see how useful the camera was without it.

The camera plugs into an AC wall socket and comes with a very long pair of cords as well as screw downs to secure the cord to the wall to make it harder to steal. From a security camera perspective, it wouldn't take a rocket scientist to walk up to the camera and unplug it to disable it, but that aside, it does have some useful functions. You can get notifications on your phone or email every time there's either movement or sound detected. You can also decide if you want to get these notifications only when nobody is home. You can go into the Nest app and view the camera live at any time. When you get the Nest camera, they include a thirty-day free trial of the Nest Aware service where you get the notifications of movement and face detection. You can then go back and look at video of any of these events and of course switch to live viewing at any time. After the thirty-day trial, you lose the face detection but still get notifications of movement but only with fairly grainy still shot archives of what happened. Also, the number of notifications increased so much that I turned it off because it was so annoying.

So, without the subscription, I am essentially using the camera as an on-demand live video source with no archival footage. The net effect is that I am still looking for a better system for handling video. Notably, in our new home, I have not found a reasonable application for the camera, so it's currently lying dormant in a box.

Bottom Line – Home Security System

> What to Do
>
> What you end up doing with your home security system depends a lot on what your starting point is. If you already have a system that is centrally monitored and are paying more than $20 per month for the monitoring service (and your equipment is paid off), chances are you can get a much lower monthly fee by calling your provider and telling them you want to cancel the service.
>
> If you want to put in a system that also includes smartphone control, you may be able to extend the system you have, or you can opt for a new system that provides all the perimeter protection with door and window sensors, sirens, keypads, glass break detector, motion sensors, central monitoring via a cellular connection, and also smartphone control via an app. The two systems that I narrowed my search to are SimpliSafe and Abode, both of which offer high quality complete do-it-yourself security systems. SimpliSafe has a lower up-front cost for equipment but a higher monthly monitoring fee, while Abode's up-front cost is higher, with a lower monthly fee if paid annually. Abode also can integrate with other Smart Home products like smoke detectors, cameras, and sensors. I chose Abode for my Smart Home design.
>
> When it comes to cameras, I chose to do this separately from the security system, experimenting

with the Nest outdoor camera. Costs can be very high for monthly storage of video with some cameras, and a good chunk of your Internet plan can get used, so read the fine print and understand both of those sets of implications. I am waiting for a system that has the video storage done in the home in a simple and integrated way that also allows for remote access.

Budget

The biggest cost of security systems over time are the monthly fees. As an example, if a system costs $800 for all the gear and you have to pay $50 per month for remote monitoring, your ten-year total cost is $6,800. When you look at it that way, it matters little what the equipment costs because it is dwarfed by the monitoring costs. Therefore, job number one in security systems is keeping the monthly fee to a minimum. You could argue that if you have self-monitoring with your smartphone, you don't even need monitoring by a third party, but this assumes you are always available to diagnose problems and your Internet connection is always up.

New do-it-yourself systems cost between $500 and $1000, depending on how large a system you need. If you do choose a monitoring service, you shouldn't have to pay more than $20 to $25 per month.

Video surveillance cameras range in price but are typically in the $200 range. Often times there are charges to store your video in the Cloud that can be as high as $300 per year so evaluate very carefully whether you need that service or not.

Result

A security system is something that many homes have or need. In the past, large security system companies had a lock on the market with promises of free equipment in exchange for long term monitoring contracts. Now, we have choices using high quality DIY systems that you buy up front and either monitor with your smartphone or pay a lower monthly fee for monitoring. In our old home, I chose to keep my existing system and I negotiated a lower monthly fee from one of the big security companies.

For our new house, I purchased the Adobe security system with an annual monitoring plan that nets out to $20 per month. The freedom of being able to arm and disarm the system with a smartphone is super convenient but I still have a keypad for manual use. I learned that if the alarm goes off by accident and your phone starts beeping at you and you "verify" the alarm, it means you will get a visit from the police.

I'd give Abode full marks for overall functionality, but work still needs to be done on the usability front to make things simpler to configure in the notifications section. Always do the configuration with a computer and browser and manage the system day-to-day with the smartphone app.

Chapter 18 – Things Working Together

By now, you probably have a lot of devices working in your Smart Home, some of them together, and some independently controlled by their own app. As a reminder, you'll always need the native phone app to install and update whatever product you picked, but you might not use that app on a day-to-day basis for turning things on and off or setting scenes (creating a group of things that you can do something to all at once) or schedules (e.g. turn on these five lights and close five blinds at sunset every day). For example, using the Lutron app for controlling the lighting is an option but so is using the Apple Home app which can also control any other Apple HomeKit enabled products that you may have. But if you don't have an iPhone, the Apple Home app will not be relevant to you.

To add another twist, if you look at the Nest homepage, there is a huge list of works-with-Nest products that might be an option for you to experiment with. It only gets fuzzier from there because there is another class of apps, like IFTTT (IF This, Then That) and Stringify, that also tie different products together in specific ways. And to add to the mix are products like Alexa, from Amazon, Google Home, and the new Apple HomePod which are voice-activated speakers that can do many things including controlling your home devices.

Feel free to go to the various websites to see the ever-changing capabilities of some of these apps and products, but in the end, it leads to two fundamental questions:

1) Should my purchasing decision be impacted by the matrix of what works with what?
2) With all the choices out there, what should I be using to run these Smart Home systems on a day-to-day basis?

This is probably the most dynamic part of the whole Smart Home puzzle so before answering these questions, we need to understand what these integrations mean because they are not all equal. I'll provide some specific examples as well so you can see how different they are, and then let you know what I am doing now, and offer some recommendations for you.

Apple HomeKit

Some of the devices you'll buy are Apple HomeKit compatible. If they are, you can use the Apple Home app on your iPhone or iPad to control, group, and schedule any of the devices, as long as you have a newer generation Apple TV on your home network. In my case, the Lutron Caséta lighting, iDevices outdoor plugs, Schlage and Premis door locks, Ecobee thermostat, Lutron Serena shades, and MyQ garage door home bridge are all HomeKit compatible. I specifically chose smoke detectors from Nest that are not HomeKit products because they are not something I need to program to do anything on a day-to-day basis. The Abode security system is not HomeKit compatible, but it would be nice if it were. Since I have an iPhone, I use the Apple Home app to create schedules for dusk, night time, and other schedules to come. They are simple to create, so literally anyone can do this with no instruction.

There are a couple of important things to know about HomeKit compatibility. The first is that for companies to be part of the program, there is a dependency on hardware so if you buy a product that is not HomeKit compatible and hope that it will become so via a software update, (i.e. no cost to you) you would be making a mistake. A good example: The Chamberlain MyQ garage door opener was not HomeKit compatible (as of Feb 2017) but they announced it would be later in 2017. If you wanted it before then, you would either have to buy a new one later or buy a bridge from them to make it HomeKit compatible, but either way, it means more dollars out of your pocket. This is the reason I waited to buy that product until the HomeKit version was available.

The downside of this program is that it takes companies longer to join the HomeKit club than some of the others that follow, but the upside is more stringent requirements imposed by Apple, which yield a consistent, simple experience using the Apple Home app. I mentioned this earlier, but when I started out looking into Smart Home purchases, my initial inclination was to favor products that were HomeKit compatible to minimize the number of apps required to run the system day-to-day. I later realized that for certain products, it doesn't really matter if they're part of HomeKit. Case in point is the Rachio sprinkler system which has its own great app for scheduling your sprinkler zones. You *have* to use it to set up the system, and because you program it once, and then it runs on its own, there's no need for it to be tied into the Apple Home app.

My recommendation is that if you want to go the Apple HomeKit route, the gadgets that matter the most are the ones that you would want to schedule on a day-to-day basis and are mostly of the on/off variety of devices. (Lights, plugs, blinds, door locks, garage door opener, thermostat etc.)

Two more things about HomeKit to note. I mentioned that the Lutron Caséta lighting products are HomeKit compatible. To be more precise, it is actually the Lutron Bridge that is HomeKit compatible as it translates the proprietary Lutron Clear Connect protocol spoken by all the dimmers and blinds to the Internet. Lutron doesn't make the only bridge that speaks Clear Connect. Wink also makes a Hub called the Wink 2 Hub of all things, that can be used in place of the Lutron Bridge. (Hub and Bridge are used somewhat interchangeably here). BUT, the Wink Hub doesn't have

HomeKit compatibility so this means if you use the Wink Hub for your Lutron gear, you can use the Lutron app (or the Wink app - more on that in a bit) but not the Apple Home app.

The last fairly obvious thing to note is that if you don't have an iPhone or iPad, the whole HomeKit thing is not relevant to you. Chances are, the next sections are areas you have already been experimenting with, so let's dive into those now.

Works with Nest

Nest makes a number of different products including thermostats, smoke detectors, and cameras, with others likely to come over time. They have a *Works with Nest* program that you can read about on their website where manufacturers of other products can put a "Works with Nest" sticker on their product and it will be compatible with Nest products. In contrast to Apple's HomeKit, the Nest integrations are all done in software which means their product list is a lot longer and changes almost weekly as new products come out and new capabilities get released with software updates. What does this really mean though? The short answer is that it depends on the product and which of the Nest products they have chosen to work with. The full detail of the exact integration is shown on the Works with Nest tab on the Nest web page but here are a few examples for illustrative purposes.

- The Rachio Sprinkler controller will cycle on your outdoor sprinklers if the Nest Smoke detector goes off inside the house.
- The Chamberlain MyQ Garage door opener will work with the Nest camera to provide alerts when your garage door is open or closed. And you can also use the MyQ app to see your Nest thermostat temperature and set your home/away status.
- You can use Amazon's Alexa to send voice commands to change the temperature on your Nest thermostat.

There are plenty of apps that also work with Nest in the context of being able to control the Nest Thermostat from within another app. The earlier example of the Lutron app is one as is the Wink app to be explained later. You can probably see that some of these integrations are more useful than others so the moral of this story is that the "Works with Nest" logo can mean very different things, and you have to go to the Nest web site to learn exactly what that integration is to know whether this would change your opinion as to which device you should buy. Because Nest has a number of very different products, Works with Nest really means that at least *one* of the Nest products works with your product or app of interest, not necessarily all of them. Also note that you can buy a product that has no Nest integrations but later, a free software update could enable it.

Obviously, none of this matters if you have no Nest products, but for me, I consider any Nest integrations more of a bonus feature that I might want to use rather than something I specifically look for when choosing a product. Most companies that ship quality products will want to tie themselves to as many "works with" programs as possible because they have to hedge their bets on who the winners are in the Smart Home space.

Works with Alexa

Amazon makes a number of home voice recognition products ranging in price from $40 to $180. One is the Echo, the size of a large beer can, which has a good quality integrated speaker and the other is the Dot, about the size of a hockey puck and functionally similar to the Echo but with only a tiny speaker, not particularly great for playing music. There is also a mid-range portable version called the Tap with more likely to come over time. All of them are sometimes called Alexa because that is the code word to wake up the unit to ask it to do something. "Alexa, what time is it?" If you have an iPhone, it is roughly the equivalent of Siri but more programmable via the use of what Amazon calls skills. It is well beyond the scope of this book to list all of the things that Alexa can do, but one of them is to control some of your Smart Home devices. Which ones? It depends on whether they are part of the works with Alexa program and the exact functions you can do depend on what the company with the product wants you to be able to do.

For example, the Rachio sprinkler controller has at least 140 different commands that you can ask Alexa to do. Lutron, Nest, and iDevices also have integrations with Alexa and because this is all done in the apps in software, this list is likely to grow without your having to change any hardware. The way to link your devices to Alexa is to use your Alexa Phone app (or using the Alexa web page on your computer) and enable skills for each of the products you want to control. It looks a lot like adding an app to the Alexa app but once you do the first one, you will see that it is pretty intuitive. Once the Lutron lighting is added for example, you can just tell Alexa to turn on the living room light and bingo, it will come on. Alexa, of course, does many other useful things that have nothing to do with Smart Home control, but I will leave it to you to explore that on your own.

What does the Smart Home Professor make of all this coolness? First, in order to use it effectively for controlling devices, you have to remember what you named them all (outside lights is not the same as outdoor lights or back outdoor lights or outdoor back lights) in order for Alexa to do what you want. Second, the Dot and Echo Alexa models are plugged into the wall so that means if you want to have voice control in every room, you are going to need to buy one of the models for each room. Also, anyone's voice can trigger Alexa, so if your kid or even a voice on the TV says for Alexa to turn on the air conditioning to 60° Fahrenheit, then she will do it if that skill is enabled. If you are using the Apple Home app, you already have this type of functionality using Siri on your iPhone which only works with your own voice, so you may or may not need both types of voice control.

Alexa is definitely a cool product and I had her set up to control my home devices but I rarely use her, mostly because I don't remember what I called anything. Again, I don't think works with Alexa is a buying criteria for any of the products I would choose and like the works with Nest program, it is more of a bonus to play with and impress friends.

Wink

As mentioned in various chapters including HomeKit section, one of the big questions to answer is what is the main app going to be that controls the bulk of your Smart Home experience. Certainly, you can run with one app per product, but creating scenes and schedules, which is one of the most powerful aspects of Smart Home, means that you'll want to have at least one candidate to take over this role. This is exactly the spot that Wink is vying to establish itself, so it is not surprising that the Wink Hub is not HomeKit compatible since they are effectively competing against Apple for this role.

Wink's main product is a Hub (aka Bridge) that converts all the Smart Home languages (Z-Wave, ZigBee, Lutron Clear Connect, Bluetooth LE) back into your home network so that everything can be connected. It then also supplies a phone app that you can run to orchestrate many of your things working together. The Wink web site has a running list of all the products that it supports and naturally that will also change over time. Incidentally, from the ones that I chose to use, many are on the list like Lutron lighting and blinds, Nest thermostat and smoke detectors, Schlage door lock, MyQ garage door opener, Ring doorbell, Rachio sprinklers, and Alexa. But what does this really mean? I don't have a Wink Hub so what happens if I just install the Wink app and see what works?

What shows up in the Wink app depends on two things. The first is how a given device is connected to your network. If it's connected by WiFi and doesn't need to go through a bridge (which in this case means a bridge that isn't the Wink bridge), then there is a chance it will appear in the Wink app. Examples of things that I have installed that are connected by WiFi and show up in the Wink app: The Rachio Sprinkler Controller, Nest thermostat, Nest smoke detector, Ring doorbell, but not the iDevices outdoor switch. Why not iDevices? That is the second dependency; the device also has to allow itself to be controlled by having a programming interface and Wink has to choose to add that specific device. In the case of iDevices, either there is no programming interface or Wink has decided not to add it yet.

If you look in the Wink app, the Lutron lighting and Schlage lock (neither WiFi-connected directly) both show up as supported devices but because I am not using the Wink Hub, it does not support either of those products in my home setup. Recall that the Lutron products talk a language called Lutron Clear Connect and are bridged to the main network using a HomeKit compatible Lutron Bridge. Also, the Schlage Lock is connected using Bluetooth LE back to the AppleTV. If I bought the Wink Hub (approx. $100), then these two products would also be integrated with Wink at the cost of losing use of the Apple Home app.

This might seem like too much complexity, and in my opinion, it is, but I am showing Wink as one alternative example as an overall app that can run many of the devices for day-to-day use. Certainly, if you don't use an iPhone and therefore have no need for Apple HomeKit, this is an option worth considering. The number of devices supported over time will hopefully increase with new software releases and new product releases from various vendors. Do remember though that you will still need to have each and every product app on your phone anyways for doing firmware updates and any troubleshooting should something go wrong. Also, complex apps like the Rachio sprinkler app are only partially implemented in Wink so it may just be easier to use the native Rachio app since it is not something you would need to use on a daily basis anyway.

IFTTT and Stringify

IFTTT (IF This, Then That) and Stringify are similar phone apps that perform unifying Smart Home functions but on a much broader scale than just Smart Home. For simplicity reasons, only the Smart Home part will be explained.

IFTTT is a collection of Applets, or tiny programs, that people have written that do very specific things. For example, there is one that turns on the Lutron lights if there is a smoke alarm emergency from a Nest smoke detector. If you were to click on this, it would require you to provide your login to both Lutron and Nest in order to activate the Applet. If you have some other brand of smoke detector or lighting or want something else slightly different to happen, then you have to find a different Applet that does exactly what you want with exactly what you have.

There are literally hundreds if not thousands of Applets all available within the IFTTT app that you can search for to see if there are some combinations that suit your needs. Remember to check for all the non-Smart Home functions too. There are lots of other things like getting notifications from ESPN with your team's final score or sending out a tweet when the season changes on Mars. And if you really want to get creative, you can create your own Applet using the app which can potentially do something very unique to your situation.

Stringify is similar to IFTTT and uses something called flows. A flow is simply a command to do something, when something else happens; called a trigger and an action. For example, every night at 9:00pm, you can trigger a weather report for tomorrow as a notification on your phone. There are some generic default "Things" that will get you started, but you can add things like your Smart Home products including Nest, Rachio, Alexa, Ring, and even IFTTT, that can be used as triggers or actions. With Stringify, you are creating your own flows to make things happen so you are only limited by your imagination and the products that Stringify supports. Like IFTTT, this involves much tinkering around so if you don't have the time but do have the desire, ask your nine-year-old to help. It's probably better than them watching TV and maybe they will get interested in programming and depart your payroll before the age of twenty-five.

Now, back to our questions from the beginning of this chapter.

1) Should a purchasing decision be impacted by the matrix of what works with what?

If you plan on using an iPhone to run your Smart Home system on a day-to-day basis, then the answer is yes, you will want to have as many of the smart devices be HomeKit compatible as possible. If you are planning on using an Android device, it is still a good idea to choose an overall app like Wink or a competitor to run the majority of devices. In this case, try the various apps out there vying for this position, and then select your products based on which app you have chosen.

2) With all the choices out there, what should I be using to run these Smart Home systems on a day-to-day basis?

Like the answer to the last question, use the Apple Home app with all your HomeKit compatible products if you plan on using an iPhone. For specialized products like sprinkler systems and video doorbells or products that you don't interact with daily like smoke detectors, use the app that comes with that product.

Whether using an iPhone or Android device to run your home, the goal should always be simplicity and minimizing the number of apps that you need to create schedules and interactions. This will take some experimentation on your part to achieve this goal in the Android world.

Apps like IFTTT and Stringify are also useful to fill some stopgap holes when you need two different products being controlled by 2 different apps to interact in some specific way.

Bottom Line - Things Working Together

What to Do

If you are an iPhone user, your best bet is to get products that are HomeKit compatible and they will all show up in the Apple Home app which allows for easy scheduling and automation. Some products that don't require daily interaction like smoke detectors don't really need to be in the HomeKit mix so you can pick the one you like the best overall. Other specialized products like the Rachio sprinkler controller are so unique that it is also not so critical that they are controlled by the Apple Home app.

The Android world is a bit more complicated but choosing another overall app like Wink is still a good idea. Choose one that has the most products supported and make sure you try out the actual app you plan to use to ensure that all the functionality you need is still there. There is no question that this requires more time and experimentation than the Apple approach.

Sometimes, you will want your Smart Home products to interact with things outside their known environment, and apps like IFTTT and Stringify are ideal for setting up these custom interactions. Maybe you want to change the color of your smart bulbs when your favorite sports team wins a game, or turn on your Christmas lights when it is snowing. If so, these apps are ideal to create custom interactions.

Chapter 19 – Moving with a Smart Home

When I wrote the first draft of this book, I had no idea that all the Smart Home goodness I was putting into my home would soon be someone else's. The moment I put the finishing touches on that draft, we sold the house and bought a new one.

I massively underestimated the effort involved in transferring my Smart Home over to its new owner. I wanted to make sure that I safely decoupled myself from all digital control of the old home and made it simple for the buyer to reap the benefits of their new Smart Home right away.

This chapter isn't just for people selling their home, buying a new home, or real estate agents. It's for everyone. Implementing Smart Home technology correctly out of the gate will make real estate transactions simple and smooth for the seller, buyer and agents.

More and more people have some Smart Home products in their home and as people move around, it's important to make sure that the buyer and seller add these new steps to their list:

1) Determine which Smart Home products will stay with the house and which will leave with the seller.
2) Ensure the seller unhooks themselves from the Smart Home products that are being left behind.
3) Make it easy for the buyer to get inherited Smart Home products up and running.

What Stays and What Goes?

The general rule is that anything that is attached to the house stays in a sale, otherwise the seller may take it. If there is any doubt, specify everything in an addendum to the sales contract.

You would typically leave behind controllers for pool equipment, outdoor sprinkler systems, in-wall light switches, smart bulbs, thermostats, smoke detectors, video doorbell, cameras (if wired in), security system, window blinds, garage door opener, and door locks.

Products that would leave with the seller would typically be the modem, router(s), lamp dimmers, outdoor on/off plug adapters, music system, AppleTV, Smart Home bridges, and any other sensors not attached to the home (like water leak detectors).

You can immediately see the consequences of a poorly executed transfer. If the seller doesn't "disconnect" him/herself from the Smart Home products that are staying, the buyer won't have control over them. In fact, the seller will maintain control of the old Smart Home equipment when network connectivity is re-established. As a buyer, you don't want someone raising and lowering your thermostat remotely.

Also, the seller will be taking much of the equipment (router, bridges etc.) required to make the whole Smart Home system work, so if the buyer doesn't know how to set it all back up, they lose out on the advantages of inheriting the Smart Home products that are staying behind. Here is how to ensure the transfer goes smoothly.

<u>Seller's Steps to Unhook from Smart Home Products Left Behind</u>

Before disconnecting any networking equipment, the seller should do the following:

1) Go into each app for every product type being left behind that uses your *personal* e-mail as an account, and delete those products from his/her app.

At the beginning of this section, I suggested that you create a new e-mail address that you will use only for that house's Smart Home accounts and devices. When you move, you just give this e-mail away to the buyer and save both of you a lot of time. The buyer just has to change the password on the e-mail and Smart Home accounts tied to it.

The products will still operate but in standalone mode similar to the state they were in when originally installed but they will no longer be associated with the app on the seller's phone.

2) For products that need to continue to operate on a schedule, like pool controllers, sprinkler systems, and video doorbells, create a new e-mail address and password and link these systems to that new e-mail and away from the seller's personal mail. Give the new e-mail and password to the buyer so that they can use it to get these up and running again.

3) If you had the foresight to have created a portable e-mail account to tie your Smart Home to, remove your name as the contact and write down all the passwords for the buyer.

4) Disconnect everything that you are taking and get ready to install it at your new home. At this point, the seller would have no control over any of the former Smart Home devices being left behind, even when things are reconnected.

Because I didn't have a separate e-mail for Smart Home gear in the old house, it took me almost eight full hours to unhook myself and then hook the buyer up to a new e-mail address. Selling a home is stressful enough that this added work is hopefully something that you can avoid.

How a Buyer Re-establishes Smart Home Functionality

There are two things the buyer needs to know to get things back up and running. First, you have to know which products being left behind are Smart Home capable. Second is the knowhow to set up the Internet, Network, which apps to use to run everything, and what to buy to fill in the gaps for the products that were taken by the seller.

This is where the Smart Home savvy real estate agents can play a new, key role in the transaction. On the next page is a snapshot of a one-page checklist that a real estate agent can use to keep track of which Smart Home products the buyer will have to work with. A full-page fillable PDF version is available on the smarthomeprofessor web site.

Smarthome Checklist for Realtors

Courtesy: Smarthome Professor
www.smarthomeprofessor.com

Property:	Street Address	
	City	
Selling Agent:	Name	
	Phone	
	e-mail	

List of Smarthome Devices to Stay in the Home

	Quantity	Device Type	Brand	Special Instructions
1		Dimmer Switches		
2		On/Off Switches		
3		AC Outlets		
4		Smart Bulbs		
5		Thermostats		
6		Smoke Detectors		
7		Outdoor Sprinkler Controller		
8		Door Locks		
9		Garage Door Opener		
10		Door Bell		
11		Pool Equipment Controller		
12		Window Blinds		
13		Home Security Alarm		
14		Security Camera		
15		Ceiling Fans		
16		Hot Water Heater		
17		Heating / Air Conditioning		
18		Appliances		
19		Solar		

Only list smarthome items that are controllable with a smartphone or computer

In most cases, the best way to remove these devices from the seller's phone App is to have them go into each App and remove all the devices while their network is still up and running

Give a copy of this to the Buyer so that they know which Apps to download to set up their new smarthome

The seller's agent should have the seller fill this out in detail and provide it to the buyer's agent. If the selling agent does not provide a list of the Smart Home products, the buyer should insist on getting this before finalizing any buying arrangement.

If the buyer receives this sheet, they will know what they have to work with. If the seller doesn't fill this out, then the buyer can go hunting around the house for these types of Smart Home products and make their own checklist.

Unless the seller has provided all the details of how to get all the existing Smart Home products up and running, the buyer should assume that other than the physical installation of the products, they are starting from scratch in terms of the apps and programming. It will be necessary to reset each product to factory defaults and start each install from the beginning. This is of course after you get your network infrastructure in place.

> If you move into a home with Smart Home technology, assume that you will have to factory reset all of the products and start programming from scratch. It's not as hard as it sounds and you will learn all about each product at the same time!

This book will be a great gift for anyone buying a home with Smart Home products installed, as it will walk them through everything they need to do to get their Smart Home operational.

Summary

I hope that this book has made it easier for you to make a Smart Home out of your house. There are many more devices to discover other than what I covered in this book, including smart appliances, sensors, sleep aids, baby monitors, vacuums, celling fans, etc. I tried to pick enough of the popular items so that even if you want to add more to your mix, the strategies, methods of choosing the right product, and the technology should all be familiar, so you can take your next steps with confidence. The appendices following provide a bit more insight into other technical topics and may prove valuable if you choose to expand your system.

As noted many times throughout this book, there will be many technology, product, and company changes over time so the companion web site at www.smarthomeprofessor.com will keep you up to date with any new discoveries.

Lastly, have fun with this. Once you start, it tends to be addictive, so just take it one step at a time.

Appendix 1 – More Tech Details

The previous chapter touched a bit on some of the languages and protocols that Smart Home devices use, since they are not all connected to the network using WiFi. The main reason that other wireless protocols are used is that many of the small devices like sensors, window contacts and others, operate on batteries, and it is a goal to try and extend that battery life as long as possible. WiFi is not known for its lengthy battery life so you rarely see it used on battery powered gadgets used in the Smart Home.

Each of the different wireless protocols that you are likely to encounter is described below, noting their key characteristics. The next section on bridges will explain how to connect, or bridge, these protocols to ones that your network and smartphone can understand.

Protocols

Lutron ClearConnect

Lutron developed a wireless protocol for their devices that uses an interference free radio band for communication with one another. It is a so-called hub-and-spoke design, meaning that all of the devices communicate back with the central hub (in my case the Lutron Bridge), which is plugged into the router. This allows the system to be very responsive to commands, like turning off a bunch of lights at once and having them all do so in synch. It's used in all the Lutron Caséta lighting products and the Serena blinds. They also published a detailed white paper explaining the inner workings of Clear Connect and have licensed the technology to other companies to include in their bridges.

Bluetooth Low Energy (BTLE or BLE)

BLE is a standard available on many products including your smartphone, computer, many fitness products, speakers, etc. The Low Energy version of Bluetooth is a lower data rate than standard Bluetooth and is suitable for sending small amounts of data, for example sending commands from an Apple TV to a door lock to tell it to lock or to check its status.

Z-Wave

Z-Wave is a wireless protocol released in 2004 by a Danish company called Zensys, later acquired in 2009 by Sigma Designs, that is used for signaling and communication by home automation devices. Z-Wave uses a so-called mesh topology where sensors can communicate back to the main hub through other sensors. This tends to make the coverage a bit easier if you have a lot of devices at the expense of some added delay if you have to take a number of hops to get back to the hub or bridge. There are thousands of products using Z-Wave and many bridges that support it as well.

ZigBee

ZigBee is another wireless protocol that has been standardized by the IEEE (an international standards body), the same group that created the WiFi standards. It is also targeted for low data rate, long battery life home sensor products. It has been around since 2004 and supports the same topology as Z-Wave and for all intents and purposes is an alternative of Z-Wave. A quick check shows a number of Smart Home products available with ZigBee but probably not as many as with Z-Wave.

The key question about all these protocols is whether the protocol supported by a device you are looking to buy should influence your buying decision. The short answer is no, it is much better to focus on getting the best products for the job but knowing what protocols they support is important. If the device is WiFi, you know how to do the test to determine if it is likely to work in the place you want to install it. If it supports BLE like the Schlage and Kwikset door locks do, you know that it has to connect back to something that also supports BLE, namely the Apple TV. If it is either Z-Wave or ZigBee, you will have to connect those back to a bridge that supports those protocols. If you built out your Smart Home exactly like the book outlined, only the Abode gateway (home security system) supports Z-Wave or ZigBee and acts as a bridge for those protocols. Recall that the Lutron products all use Clear Connect and so the Lutron bridge that we installed in the lighting section would be available to connect other Clear Connect products.

Now it is time to look at a few bridges in the event that you do have other products that use Z-Wave or ZigBee. As mentioned regarding the Abode products for home security, the Abode gateway (or the central unit) is also a Z-Wave and ZigBee bridge, one of the reasons that I chose this for the security system for the new home. It allows expansion for other products that they don't sell, like leak detectors, freeze sensors, and others.

Bridges

There are a number of companies that make bridges (aka hubs) supporting multiple protocols. Wink for example has a bridge that supports Clear Connect, BLE, Z-Wave and ZigBee, but not Apple HomeKit. Samsung-owned SmartThings has a ZigBee and Z-Wave hub as well and a list of compatible products. Other vendors are Insteon, Iris, and WeMo. A handy comparison chart of what is supported by all of these hubs is available at http://www.insteon.com/technology/#systemscompared. From the chart, you can see that Insteon uses its own protocol, but also has a HomeKit enabled Hub. Iris uses Z-Wave and WeMo by Belkin uses WiFi.

So, what to make of all this? In my opinion, buy the best products and work backwards and source a hub if you need one. Always try to plug them into the Ethernet ports on your main router as opposed to one of the extenders. I favor a multi-vendor approach to keep from being locked in to or dependent on the survival of any one vendor. Also, unless all these companies merge, I highly doubt that you will find all the best products in each category from one manufacturer alone. As you have likely concluded by now, keeping things simple is a good idea by minimizing the number of apps required to run your Smart Home day-to-day.

Appendix 2 – Evaluating What to Buy

Deciding which Smart Home gadget to buy within a certain category is half the battle in your Smart Home project. I started mine with lighting and it certainly was not clear at all to me how to approach the dizzying number of choices in order to find something that works for all requirements. This whole ecosystem of Smart Home systems is a multi-vendor endeavor by definition, but I remain convinced that a simple ease of use experience is what the end consumer will demand before the market really takes off. So, to that end, a quick analysis of the Smart Home market is in order, as this will influence some purchasing and other strategic app choices.

Smart Home Market Analysis

There are some vendors who make specific Smart Home products to solve specific problems. Areas such as lighting, outdoor sprinkler systems, security systems, cameras, door locks, blinds, thermostats, smoke detectors, hot water heaters, and music systems are examples. In most cases, in order to make a truly great product in any of these markets, it takes a tremendous amount of focus, dedication, time, and money to get it right. You might expect the best Smart Home door lock to come from a traditional lock manufacturer for example. On the other hand, some markets are ripe for a new way of doing things and have attracted startup companies that push the incumbents. In either case, it seems unlikely that in the next three to five years that any one company will have all of the pieces necessary for a solid Smart Home design.

There is another set of vendors who focus less on making the individual products and more on creating infrastructure that allows it all to work together seamlessly. Some of these companies like Vivint are more focused on offering this integration as a service and making their money from monthly fees. Other companies such as Apple are interested in making you more dependent on their smartphone and tablet products, making their money on upgrades to newer, more functional products.

The third class of company is a hybrid of the two, where they supply some of the products but also create an open environment where their products tie in nicely to others, but also provide a way to use and manage as many of the products as possible. A good example of this is Wink, who sells a hub that integrates products using many different wireless technologies and also has an app to manage (most) of them.

Another interesting company is Google. As of this writing in late 2017, Google has two distinct Smart Home stores. The first one is the Nest store that makes and sells thermostats, video cameras, and smoke detectors along with products from Google (the other part of Google) and many third-party vendors that all integrate with Nest. The other store is the Google store, and it sells smartphones, streaming video, a speaker assistant, tablet computer, and a few other things. If you step back a bit, they are starting to look more and more like Apple and certainly have the money to merge their efforts and become a dominant player both in the gadgets themselves and getting them all to work together. Whether they take this step or not is anyone's guess, but I wouldn't be surprised to see a huge Smart Home push from them.

Regardless if you are a fan of Apple, Google, or the underdog startup (who often gets acquired by one of these giants anyway), there is no way to tell who the dominant player is going to be, but my money is that it will be one of these two. And of course, we can't ever count Amazon out, either. In addition to innovating in a number of technology areas, I still believe Amazon is the best place to get reliable data on the quality of products available in the marketplace.

Using Amazon Ratings

There will be many times you are looking to find the right product and there just is no clear and obvious choice. Using some specific examples, we'll walk through how you can use product ratings on amazon.com to help you decide.

The first two things to look at are the quantity of reviews, which is an indication of overall sales relative to the competitor, and the percentage of 5 star reviews. Here are three examples of top products in their category: Sonos Play:1, Rachio Sprinkler, and the Nest thermostat.

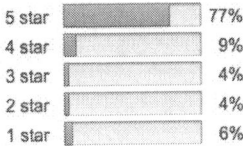

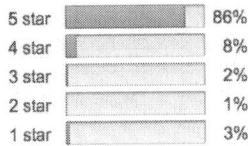

Customer Reviews	Customer Reviews	Customer Reviews
★★★★⯪ 2,904	★★★★⯪ 1,229	★★★★⯪ 11,286
4.6 out of 5 stars ▾	4.7 out of 5 stars ▾	4.6 out of 5 stars ▾
5 star 77%	5 star 86%	5 star 87%
4 star 9%	4 star 8%	4 star 8%
3 star 4%	3 star 2%	3 star 1%
2 star 4%	2 star 1%	2 star 1%
1 star 6%	1 star 3%	1 star 3%

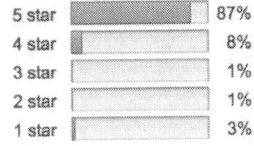

All have thousands of reviews and ratings in the high fours with near 80% or over five star ratings, our goal in selecting quality products. These are all excellent products and with the large number of ratings, you can use this data to feel confident in your selection.

Now, here are the ratings of three of the major players in the video doorbell product category: Ring Pro, Skybell, and August.

Customer Reviews

⭐⭐⭐⭐☆ 5,315

4.1 out of 5 stars ▾

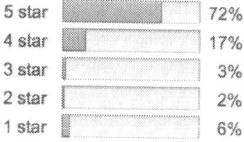

5 star	72%
4 star	17%
3 star	3%
2 star	2%
1 star	6%

Customer Reviews

⭐⭐⭐☆☆ 564

3.6 out of 5 stars ▾

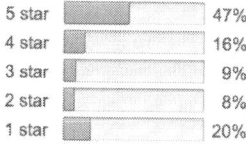

5 star	47%
4 star	16%
3 star	9%
2 star	8%
1 star	20%

Customer Reviews

⭐⭐⭐☆☆ 316

2.9 out of 5 stars ▾

5 star	49%
4 star	13%
3 star	6%
2 star	7%
1 star	25%

The first thing you notice is the massive difference in the quantity of product sold between the three choices. Clearly Ring Pro is dwarfing the others in sales at this point in time. But you can also tell that the overall maturity of the product is not quite there as compared to the ratings of other products like Sonos, Rachio, and Nest, all of which have exceptional products and support. Products that are clear winners have lots of reviews, and are somewhere in the 80% range giving five stars. As of this writing, Ring has 72%, Skybell has 47%, and August has 49% five star ratings. Compare this to Sonos at 77% for its Play:1 product, Rachio at 86%, and Nest Thermostat at 87%. It tells me that Ring is the leader in video door bells but it may still require some work to compare quality wise with some of the others that I know are top notch.

Pure quantity of sales and ratings don't always tell the whole story though. If you want to know why one product has a much lower overall rating, read some of the reviews and you will get a pretty quick indication of why this is the case. Sometimes the issue may just be its price so if that doesn't matter to you, then you can discount some of those reviews. If there are quality issues, people will let you know what they are. The most useful reviews are the ones that give specifics about shortcomings so again, you can determine if these issues are relevant to you.

Is using Amazon ratings a better way to evaluate products than looking for web sites that do professional evaluations? The Smart Home Professor thinks so but I still use some of the sites linked from my website as they are useful to inform us about new products coming to the market. But I trust real users like you to let the masses know how well something works in the real world so I always end up checking the Amazon ratings.